# That One Idea

*Mr. Woodard is, and is not, a remarkable man.*
*He is uncompromising, stiff, resolute – some people*
*might say obstinate.*

*He is a man of one idea, but he pursues that one idea*
*with unflagging energy and*
*considerable savoir faire.*

**Saturday Review 1853**

# That One Idea

## NATHANIEL WOODARD
## AND HIS SCHOOLS

Leonard and Evelyn
Cowie

THE WOODARD CORPORATION

First published in Great Britain 1991
The Woodard Corporation
Ellesmere, Shropshire
SY12 0EY

*Line drawings by*
DENNIS FLANDERS RWS RBA

*Design and Production by*
ESDON FROST

The Woodard Corporation would like to thank:

The Society for Promoting Christian Knowledge for their co-operation
in the compilation of this book.

The heads and staff of the schools for providing information and photo-
graphs. The pictures come from many sources and have been collected
over a period of many years, and we are not able to trace and acknowledge them individually. We are grateful to all the photographers who
have wittingly and unwittingly contributed to this commemorative
volume.

The illustrations have been selected to suggest collectively the variety
of academic, artistic, sporting and social activities that take place at
Woodard schools, as a whole. They should not be regarded competi-
tively or as necessarily reflecting the typical or main interests of any
particular school.

*British Library Cataloguing in Publication Data*

Cowie, Leonard
That one idea: Nathaniel Woodard and his
schools.
I. Title II. Cowie, Evelyn E.
III. Woodard Corporation
370.92

ISBN 0 951 76540 X

Typeset by Rowland Phototypesetting Ltd
Bury St Edmunds, Suffolk
Printed in Great Britain by
Simmons Printers Ltd, Chelmsford, Essex

# *Contents*

# The Woodard Schools

THE KING'S SCHOOL

QUEEN MARY'S

QUEEN ETHELBURGA'S

QUEEN MARGARET'S

ELMSLIE

ST JAMES

ST HILARY'S

RANBY HOUSE

WORKSOP

DENSTONE

ST ELPHIN'S

ELLESMERE

DERBY HIGH

SMALLWOOD MANOR

PRESTFELDE

ST MARY AND ST ANNE

CAWSTON

PETERBOROUGH HIGH

BLOXHAM

THE BISHOP OF HEREFORD'S BLUECOAT SCHOOL

THE ARCHBISHOP MICHAEL RAMSEY SCHOOL

THE CATHEDRAL SCHOOL

ARDINGLY

GRENVILLE

KING'S COLLEGE KING'S HALL

ST MICHAEL'S

HURSTPIERPOINT

LANCING

ST MARGARET'S

ST CLARE

# *Foreword*

BY THE
BISHOP OF WINCHESTER
PRESIDENT OF THE WOODARD
CORPORATION

*'Nathaniel Woodard, Clerk in Holy Orders, sometime Canon of Manchester, who was called to his rest on the 25th day of April, 1891, and whose body lies buried at Lancing College, founded this Corporation in the faith and fear of Almighty God, for the love of his Church, and the good of his country.'*

These opening words of the Preamble, read at every annual Chapter meeting of the Woodard Corporation, testify to the Founder's vision and achievement in providing a broad-based and distinctively Christian education for children of the middle classes.

As a parish priest working in London in the 1840s Woodard had been shocked by the ignorance, irreligion and dishonesty of what he called 'the trades class'. Earlier in the century the National Society had pioneered the foundation of Christian schools to serve the needs of the poor. Woodard believed that a comparable initiative was needed for the education of the middle classes. 'The poor cannot be successfully educated, or really benefited, unless you educate their employers,' he wrote in 1849. He therefore sought 'to provide a good and complete education for the middle classes at such a charge as will make it available for most of them'. Pupils were to be taught the fear and honour of God according to the doctrines of the Catholic Faith as set forth in the Prayer Book of the Church of England.

Woodard enlisted an impressive group of supporters to help him in his task and he succeeded in raising large sums of money. In his own life time he established eight

1

schools, and the Corporation he founded has subsequently built and acquired many more. Today there are
twenty four schools belonging to the Corporation, with
eight associated schools.

The Corporation is grateful to Leonard and Evelyn
Cowie for writing for the Centenary of Woodard's death
this account of Nathaniel Woodard's achievement and the
subsequent history of the Woodard schools. Its publication is timely and helps us to reappraise the Founder's
ideals and reaffirm the Corporation's commitment in its
schools to educational excellence, concern for the well-
being of society, and the maintenance of Christian faith
and practice.

Colin Winton

# Introduction

The history of the Woodard Corporation and its schools has previously been the subject of two books. K. E. Kirk, *The Story of the Woodard Schools* (1937, rev. ed. 1952), outlined the progress of the movement with special reference to its underlying ideals and the place of religion in its schools. Brian Heeney, *Mission to the Middle Classes: The Woodard Schools 1848–1891* (1969), is a detailed study of the work of Nathaniel Woodard in founding and organizing his schools.

This new history commemorates the centenary of Woodard's death. As well as including an account of his life and work and of the development of the Corporation by means of its central and divisional organizations, it shows how the movement has contributed to the English educational scene through its incorporated and associated schools and what plans it has for the future.

It gives considerable space to the individual schools, which are the life-blood of the Corporation. It tells their history, set against the background of the five divisions in the country, and describes how they are facing present-day circumstances. Some of these schools have already published their own histories, while others have only short articles and reminiscences of former pupils in school magazines. All, however, have valuable resources and archives, which have recently been usefully catalogued by Mr Hugh Dillon, as have those of the central and divisional offices also. The use of these records of both the schools and the administration of the Corporation has enabled us to place their histories within the wider story of the movement. We are very grateful to the Heads, Librarians and others at the schools and to all at the Central Registry and the Provincial Registries for the ready and careful help they have given us while we have been pursuing our inquiries.

*That One Idea*

This has made it possible for us to write, however briefly, about the varied origins of these schools and the way in which they have grown and are continuing to give expression to the Woodard tradition in their life and work. Inevitably it will be felt that we might have written at greater length and that we have omitted events and persons in their history which should have been included, but we have tried to do the most that our space permits, and some schools have fewer records than others. We hope that what we have done will be of interest to pupils and parents and others who wish to know more about these important schools. We hope also that it will stimulate further interest in them and encourage the writing of fuller and more detailed histories about them.

Leonard and Evelyn Cowie

4

# Nathaniel Woodard

Nathaniel Woodard was born on 21 March 1811 at Basildon Hall in Essex, the ninth of twelve children of a country gentleman unable to afford, during the agricultural depression after the Napoleonic Wars, to send them to school. Nathaniel was brought up as an Evangelical by his mother, who he said was a 'pious and devout woman'. He also was attracted by church music. He went to services, arriving home late, for which, he said he had often 'smarted for things of the sense'. It was perhaps through his mother and these services that he received his call to ordination. He prepared himself to go to university by studying under a clergyman in Norfolk and then while supporting himself as a tutor in a family. Two aunts are believed to have paid for him to go to Oxford, where he entered Magdalen Hall (now Hertford College) in 1834.

Little is known about him at Oxford. He took only a pass degree in 1840, but he had married in 1836 and had three children by 1839. It is said that the 'responsibilities of a husband and father' prevented him from 'keeping his terms with regularity and distracted his mind from prescribed studies'. Oxford, however, influenced his religion. As an Evangelical, his outlook was Protestant when he went there, but this was during the spread of the Tractarian Movement, which wished to revive an understanding of the continuity of the Church in faith and worship with its early and medieval past. Then, as R. W. Church, its historian, wrote, 'The ideas, which had laid hold so powerfully on a number of leading minds in the University, began to work with a spell'; and Woodard felt that spell.

This, however, brought him trouble. He was ordained in 1841 by the Bishop of London, Charles J. Blomfield, and made curate-in-charge of the newly-formed St Bartholomew's district in Bethnal Green, then on the edge of London. He worked hard, visiting his people, completing the church and establishing a parochial school. In May 1843 he preached in favour of the provision in the Prayer Book for confession and absolution. This controversial Tractarian view brought a complaint to the bishop, who required to see his sermon. It had such tactless phrases 'an inefficient, Godless clergy'. The Bishop condemned its 'erroneous and dangerous notions'. He was not prepared to retain him in Bethnal Green when it became a parish, but sent him to be a curate at St John's Church, Clapton.

In 1846 friends secured him an appointment as curate-in-charge of New Shoreham in Sussex, then a small but growing port, trading chiefly in coal, corn and timber; but he found it congenial. He was interested in seamen because his mother had relations in the navy. The vicar, a Tractarian, held the parishes of both Old and New Shoreham, but took charge of St Nicolas's Parish Church in Old Shoreham, residing there and leaving Woodard free in his charge, a mile away. St Mary's parish church in New Shoreham was a fine medieval building with a good choir, which especially attracted him. While at Oxford his early interest in church music had been extended by his acquaintance with Thomas Helmore (a fellow-undergraduate at Magdalen Hall), who wished to revive plainsong in England, the traditional music of the medieval Church. Before arriving at New Shoreham, he instructed the choir to learn this.

Many of his parishioners were tradesmen and masters of small coasting vessels, mostly ignorant and uneducated. There was a parochial school, but it was for poor children, who were, therefore, better educated than their employers with sad results. Though the mariners had 'charge of very considerable property and not a few lives, the loss of life and property through the incompetence of persons of this kind' was, he observed, 'incredible'. They were also hostile to religion and suspected the clergy and the social classes, with whom they were associated. The Chartist and Anti-Corn Law movements at this time aroused sharp class feeling and agitation.

He had seen this in Bethnal Green and believed education was the answer. His vicar allowed him to open a small day-school for middle-class boys—'St Mary's Grammar School' —in the dining-room of New Shoreham Vicarage. Then an illness early in 1848 enabled him to publish a pamphlet, *A Plea for the Middle Classes*, urging the need for 'providing a good and complete education for the middle classes at such a charge as will make it available for most of them'. He divided this 'new army of the middle class' into three social grades and proposed separate schools for each of them, with varying fees but united into a common brotherhood. Believing that the Church had the right and duty to provide education, he wrote, 'Some look to the government for everything. For my part, in the present state of parties in the Kingdom, I heartily trust that the government will not interfere. It would be unjust.'

Many read the pamphlet. The Church's recent educational efforts had left a gap uncovered by its schools. The National Society, founded in 1811 'for the Education of the Poor in the Principles of the Established Church', by 1846 had founded 17,000 schools with nearly a million pupils. Thomas Arnold's headmastership at Rugby (1828–42) had revived the old public schools for the wealthy, but for the middle classes the grammar schools were few and inadequate.

The *Plea* was directed at churchmen, clerical and lay, who feared the religious nonconformity and political radicalism of these increasingly important classes. Woodard envisaged public schools for them, with such traditional features as the old classical curriculum and teaching in a big schoolroom. Though the *Plea* accepted day-schools, he preferred boarding-schools because 'the chief thing is to remove the children from the noxious influence of home'. He wished to teach them the Church's belief and practice as interpreted by Tractarianism: 'Education is the best and in a way the only preaching available to children.' These schools would also produce teachers to establish 'a uniformity of education for all classes', since 'till the Church educates and trains up the middle classes, she can never effectually educate the poor'.

On 1 August 1848, only five months after issuing the *Plea*, he founded, also in rented premises in New Shoreham, the Shoreham Grammar School and Collegiate Institution (soon known as St Nicolas School) to provide 'an education for the upper portion of the middle classes—sons of clergymen and gentlemen of limited means'. An Oxford graduate taught there, with an assistant for elementary subjects. There were not enough chairs for half-a-dozen of Woodard's friends when they paid a visit. It was soon renamed SS Mary and Nicolas College when the day-boys of St Mary's School ceased to attend the Vicarage. By 1851 it had a staff of five and 78 boys. In 1857 it moved into new buildings on a site bought by Woodard on the bare slope of Lancing Hill, 2 miles east of Worthing.

Meanwhile, he established other Sussex schools to supplement this 'upper school'. St John's School, founded in 1849 and moved into permanent buildings at Hurstpierpoint in 1853, was a 'middle school', for the sons of 'tradesmen, farmers, clerks, etc.'. There followed in 1858 St Saviour's School, a 'lower school', finally established at Ardingly in 1870, 'for the sons of small shopkeepers, farmers, mechanics, clerks and others of limited means'. While the diet of St Nicolas School was modelled on Winchester College, this school was fed like St Anne's Orphanage in London, which meant meat twice a week and bread and butter for breakfast and tea. These three boarding schools were an epitome of the ideas of the *Plea*.

In 1850 Woodard resigned from New Shoreham to pro-

*Nathaniel Woodard in 1870*

mote and finance his plans. By 1855 he collected about £40,000 for Hurstpierpoint, and £30,000 for Lancing during the next few years. Much of this went on the buildings. He said, 'No system of education would be perfect which did not provide for the cultivation of the taste of the pupils through the agency of the highest examples of architecture.' He employed leading architects for these buildings and chose fine sites.

He used what his admirer, W. E. Gladstone, called 'the machinery of philanthropic agitation': pamphlets, circulars, subscriptions and school events, such as dedications, stone-layings, chapel-consecrations and annual festivals. There were also public meetings in rented halls, breakfast parties (popular in Victorian times) in restaurants, and (for trustees of his ventures) 'nice luncheons'. Lord Salisbury observed, 'The definition of a trustee is a luncheon-eating animal'. Woodard once arrived last at such a gathering and declared in the doorway, 'Gentlemen, you do not use

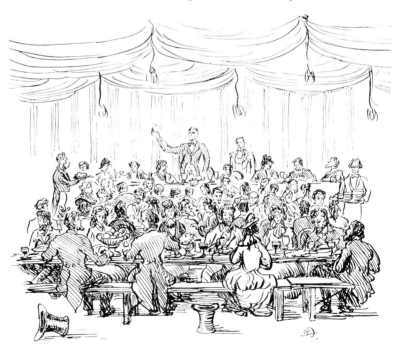

this room till you have contributed £10,000'. He got it. He once said, 'Everybody thinks it no use opposing me; even the Earl of Chichester, a Whig and an inveterate Low Churchman, told me I must succeed'.

He was slow in settling the management of his schools (see p. 13), but he always insisted that each must have a chaplain appointed by himself. Most schoolmasters then were clergymen; however, he wished a chaplain not to share in the school's teaching and discipline, but devote himself to the pastoral care of the boys, often seeing them individually 'to seek to win the children to think seriously of religious duties'. This was suspected of meaning compulsory confession, but an inquiry by the Bishop of Chichester, Ashurst T. Gilbert, exonerated the schools.

Even hostile critics had to admit that the schools upheld both religion and education. The *Brighton Gazette* in 1861 said he had 'a clever, well-devised scheme', because 'the educational advantages are made so nicely to balance the theological objections, as greatly to disarm criticism, for there will never lack parents, who, whilst recognizing the pocket advantages of the system, will be found willing enough to regard the sectarian bias as a remote contingency'.

Preoccupation with his southern schools prevented Woodard from extending his plans until in 1870, the same year in which Oxford granted him an honorary DCL, when Gladstone, then Prime Minister made him a canon of Manchester Cathedral. This took him to industrial England and carried a stipend of £2,000 a year, most of which he gave to his cause. In 1873 St Chad's School, Denstone, a 'middle school', was opened and was followed by two 'lower schools', St Oswald's School, Ellesmere (1884) and St Cuthbert's School, Worksop (1890).

His scheme ignored female education, but in 1855 he helped a girls' school in Sussex, which was destined to be a Woodard school (see p. 000). After this he said, 'So slippery are women that we must watch our progress before we promise more'. His Midland supporters, who had wider ideas, in 1874 founded St Anne's School at Abbots Bromley, the first Woodard girls' school. It was followed by St Mary's School, also in Abbots Bromley (1880), and St Winifred's School in Bangor (1887).

Woodard had also moved into the West in 1880 by buying for £8,000 a bankrupt school in Taunton, which he renamed King Alfred's School. This brought him years of financial anxiety when he was already wearied by continuous fund-raising. As his strength declined, he appointed three Regents to act for him, and after living 'in a fallen and helpless state' in Henfield, where he had resided since 1862, he died on 25 April 1891 and was buried in Lancing Chapel. By then he and his supporters had invested half a million pounds in eight boys' and three girls' schools.

# The Woodard Corporation

In 1855 Woodard vested the property of his schools in a body of trustees, but this did not provide the organization envisaged in his *Plea* (see p. 7). His first plan to have it on a diocesan basis was abandoned because some bishops mistrusted Tractarianism. In 1869 he outlined a different scheme in *A Letter to Lord Salisbury* and in 1880 drew up outline statutes for a federal body, the Corporation of SS Mary and Nicolas, but got no further. In 1893 the Corporation had to base upon his draft a constitution, which is still substantially that governing it today.

Woodard wished the country to be divided into five divisions or societies, 'one for the East, one for the West, one for the North, one for the South, and one (the most important of all) for the Midland counties'. By 1893 the Southern, Midland and Western Divisions had already been formed and so came under the new constitution. This gave each division a governing body (or Chapter), composed of a Provost and 25 Senior Fellows, 12 of whom were to be resident 'either as Head or Assistant Masters of its schools or as Chaplains, Stewards, Bursars, Organizing Secretaries or in some kindred work productive of property to the Society'. Each Division was also to have 24 Junior Fellows, who were to teach in the schools. Each Society was to elect a Provost as its head and have as its visitor the bishop of the diocese in which its central buildings were situated. The Provost and Chapter were to govern the schools and appoint the headmasters; the Provost was to appoint the chaplains of the schools. The Woodard Corporation, consisting of the Provosts and Senior Fellows of the divisions was to govern them in a federal relationship. The

Provost of the Corporation was to be the Provost of Lancing (Southern Division), who was to preside over its Corporate Chapter meetings, and in 1912 appeals were to be heard by a visitor, who was to be the bishop of the diocese in which Lancing College was situated.

Originally Woodard envisaged the Corporation, comprising both clerical and lay members, as a religious brotherhood, sustained by regular meetings and common devotions, but administration and fund-raising occupied most of its time. The finances of King's College, Taunton, dominated its early meetings—and other schools were to cause it anxiety in the future. An early decision in 1897 was to allow eucharistic vestments in school chapels with the Visitor's approval.

Over the years it had to accept changes, some of which would have worried Woodard. In 1864, for instance, he wrote to a friend, 'We may get some queer characters from the London University; and it might happen that hereafter an MA of that university might be elected Provost—an event not to be desired.'

An important development occurred in 1902 when Lancing College got control of its finances and internal government through a school committee (see p. 22). Other schools adopted these committees, at first in the Southern Division and then elsewhere, and these were replaced by School Councils from 1946. The Corporation had also to allow the teaching fellows to lapse. Woodard believed that these would establish the schools as united teaching communities, but headmasters thought they weakened their authority. Before his death he had to acknowledge their failure.

The establishment of the remaining two divisions envisaged by Woodard was slow. The Northern Division came in 1903, over ten years after his death, and the Eastern Division in 1968. Both were initiated by people inspired by the Corporation's lasting ideal of Christian education under the Church's care.

Then the Corporation was given a new legal status. The latest statutes (1980) state that each of the five divisions is a charitable company limited by its shares and managed by a Divisional Chapter, composed of the Provost and Fellows of the Division who act as the Board of Directors in a commercial company. The Chapter meets two or three times a year. The executive committee of the Chapter is the Standing Committee meeting once a term.

Each Chapter legally owns its schools and employs the staff and is also the governing body of each school, but delegates its powers to a School Council and the Headmaster and Bursar as appropriate. The chairman of the School Council is the Custos, who is usually a Fellow and a member of the Standing Committee. Each School Council has a majority of Fellows appointed by the Chapter, which also appoints other members on the nomination of the School Council itself. The Corporation is an unincorporated Society consisting of the Provosts and Fellows of the Divisions under the chairmanship of the President of the Corporation. Through its nominees the Corporate Chapter controls all the shares in the divisional companies. It defines the broad policy for the whole Corporation in spiritual, educational and financial matters.

The Corporation widened its scope in 1951 by deciding to have associated schools. These remain established by their own instrument of government, but usually have Woodard Fellows on their governing bodies. Their objects are as similar to those of the Corporation as circumstances allow. This has extended its influence to a greater variety of schools. Most of them are independent day or boarding schools, but two are maintained comprehensive schools. In 1980 it resolved to extend its relations at a 'religious, social and academic level' with these schools.

The extension of the Corporation's activities has diminished the Southern Division's predominance. In 1946 the Provost of the Corporation was replaced by an elected President. Another change occurred when a definition of the Statutes stating, 'Any word describing any officer or Fellow of the Corporation or of any Division implies a male person', was replaced by 'Words importing the masculine gender shall include the feminine;' and the Northern Division appointed the first two lady Fellows in 1970. Woodard might have liked this, since he once thought of making the Lady Warden of St Michael's School an ex-officio member of the Southern Chapter with full voting rights. A similar sign of the times was that by 1973 all boys' schools, except two, had some girls as pupils.

As the century progressed, new problems and developments arose. In 1938 concern at the 'ignorance of the Bible and Prayer Book displayed by many pupils at the schools' brought a suggestion that they should be introduced to the *Modern English Bible*. Ten years later it was reported that schools had difficulty in appointing earnest, practising teachers and in 1981 that they were producing few ordinands. In the same year the Alternative Service Book was commended to supplement the Book of Common Prayer, but the use of both was urged.

Finally, the fundamental purpose of the schools had to be considered. In 1983 a Conference of the Provost and Chaplains of the Southern Division on 'What is distinctive about the Woodard Schools?' reported that the important points were the religious training; the Eucharist as the central act of worship; a staff of professing Christians; the supportive attitude of parents; the unity provided by the Corporation; and the opportunities given to the chaplains.

# *The Southern Division*

The Woodard Corporation's very origins lie in the foundation of the Southern Division, but when was this? The Kalendars of the Corporation from 1852 to 1862 stated that the Society of SS Mary and Nicolas was formed in 1847 with the establishment of St Mary's Grammar School at Shoreham, but after that decade the date preferred has been 1 August 1848 when St Nicolas School was founded also at Shoreham. The Rev. F. M. Arnold claimed to have been appointed the first Fellow on 13 September 1848, and the Society was actually constituted in 1849 with Woodard as its first Provost.

The construction of the main quadrangle of Lancing College between 1854 and 1868 not only gave the Division its leading school. It was to be its headquarters also. Both Fellows and pupils were to worship in the Chapel, and the dining hall was nearly twice the size the College needed. It had an additional library for the Fellows, who for many years met at the College twice yearly for a week of prayer and religious study. As Woodard intended, the Society at first entirely governed the College and its later schools with a resident Provost and Fellows engaged in teaching.

The Division thus experienced Woodard's first and most intensive labours. From 1848 to 1870 he developed the complete pattern provided by the three Sussex schools—Lancing, Hurstpierpoint and Ardingly—which were intended for different social ranges and yet had a common educational and religious purpose. Here his work achieved its greatest success and most perfect form, never repeated elsewhere.

Two more schools were added to the Division—All Saints', Bloxham (1896), and St Michael's, Burton Park (1920)—and it has Tudor Hall, Banbury (1957), and the Archbishop Michael Ramsey School (1981) as associated schools. As the precursor of the Corporation's work, it has inspired and guided the later divisions and also pioneered changes adopted by them (see p. 14). A notable period of its influence began when Henry Kemble Southwell, then a canon of Truro, became Provost in 1903 and, except for a few years when he was Bishop of Lewes, held this post until his death in 1937. During that time he did much to move the schools, both in this division and the others, from their original conservative, traditional character into line with contemporary requirements in their curriculum and organization.

The Division is managed by Chapter Meetings held twice a year, in which the heads of the schools, who attend, take an important part. Though the pre-eminence of it and its Provost has declined, Lancing and its great chapel still provide the Corporation's central, unifying focus; and this is emphasized by the great annual service held there in the autumn which is attended by 3,000 people including representatives of 33 schools with their banners.

# Lancing College

SUSSEX

Woodard moved SS Mary and Nicolas College to a splendid site on a spur of the South Downs overlooking the sea to the south and the Weald to the north, comprising about 230 acres and including a college farm, which provides land for a farming group of pupils to raise a flock of sheep and other livestock. He was also, Pevsner has said, 'Lucky in his architect, R. C. Carpenter', whom he met in Bethnal Green, as he was 'almost the only person in England who could design buildings with the right mixture of competence, sincerity and common sense'. Though he died before the college moved to Lancing in 1857, when only two sides of the lower quadrangle were finished, the remaining buildings were constructed largely to his designs.

The great chapel was designed by his son, R. H. Carpenter, and begun through the efforts of Woodard's third son, Billy, in 1911. He insisted that it was built to its full height before his death, so that it would have to be completed without any reduction in the original plan. It is exceeded in height only by Westminster Abbey, York Minster and Liverpool Cathedral.

While Latin and Greek were at first the main subjects, the College also taught mathematics, music, French and German. English history was taught to the lower boys, who moved on to ancient history. As with other schools then, the school year (until 1865) was not divided into three terms but two halves: January–June and August–November. Breakfast and tea consisted of bread and butter with cocoa to drink; from Monday to Thursday dinner was roast beef with potatoes and pudding, on Friday soup and rice pudding, on Saturday 'resurrection pie' and on Sunday cold beef and cold 'milestone pudding', so-called because of its distant currants. Until 1915 beer was served at dinner and in earlier days with the bread and cheese at supper.

There were two headmasters in its first five years at Lancing. Despite further buildings, its numbers were unsatisfactory. In the first year there they rose from 77 to 97, but then fell to 76. It was small, struggling and in-efficient, unable to give, at the low fees of £30 a year for board and tuition, an education suitable for the boys whom it hoped to attract.

The Rev. R. E. Sanderson (Headmaster 1862–89) told Woodard that it was 'below all other schools of its rank and cost in the material machinery which the parents of boys, rightly or wrongly, consider essential'. Declaring it now to be 'for the sons of noblemen, clergymen, pro-fessional men and others', he said that he was determined to 'make it a public school, whole, individual and com-plete'. He raised the fees to £58, brightened the religious services, encouraged dramatic, debating and musical activities, improved the food and conditions of the boys, and raised the standard of scholarship. Termly 'Head-master's Examinations' were introduced, and bad marks were punished by a birching. Boys and masters were inspired to raise money for a gymnasium; and an Old Boy gave in 1877 studies for the VI Form, and a Great School-room out of which opened 12 classrooms, the only permanent ones until 1928. A library was opened in 1881, and in 1885 he started a modern side to teach more than the ancient languages. Numbers rose to 200, and university scholarships were gained. He was the first to emphasize the importance of sport and make all games compulsory.

Before the end of his time, however, numbers began to fall, being only 160 in 1889, partly because he did not enlarge the curriculum. He told the Schools Enquiry Commission, generally known as the Taunton Commission (1868), that science was not taught, owing to lack of time and the need to teach subjects most adapted to the pupils' future calling; he had no experience of science and admitted to a personal prejudice against it. Declining numbers were also due to the growth of preparatory schools; previously at least a third of its boys were under 14, but now it had few of them. Moreover it still lacked the comfort and care wanted by upper-class parents for their sons. In 1886 a typhoid outbreak damaged its reputation.

The new Headmaster, the Rev. H. W. McKenzie, gradually checked the falling numbers, by appointing able new masters, who developed the modern side and army class, and by improving the dormitories and sanatorium, building laboratories and making a new upper sports field out of the hillside. But an annual deficit hampered him, and he disliked the chaplain's independent position. When the Chapter did not support him, he resigned in 1894. His successor, the Rev. Dr A. J. Wilson, despite wide teaching experience, could not prevent numbers falling again, and in 1897 several Old Boys told the Chapter that its government must be changed. Finally a school committee was set up (see p. 14); but Wilson resigned in 1901, when the numbers were only 90.

The Old Boys persuaded one of their number, H. B. Tower, who was at Sedbergh, to be Headmaster and raise its prestige. The fees became a basic £73 and often more; and when he left in 1909, numbers were over 190. Money

was lacking for new buildings, but he broadened its intellectual outlook and encouraged musical and literary activities; and his sincere personal religion strengthened his influence. The College's historian, B. W. T. Handford, has said, 'The present character of Lancing dates without doubt from the time of Bernard Tower's headmastership.'

In 1909 the College Mission to Camberwell (then a very deprived and poverty-stricken area) was founded, with lasting results (see p. 57), and has since been complemented by local Community Service in the Outreach Scheme. In 1982, fifty years after the death of the explorer, Gino Watkins, who was educated at Lancing, an expedition from the College to Malawi helped to build the Malosa Secondary School, which has now 380 boys and girls, all boarders. It is linked with the Woodard Corporation, and every other year pupils go there to stay with the local people.

When the Rev. H. T. Bowlby succeeded Tower, he resolved to get the College the facilities it needed. His energy within three years gained another sports field, a new sanatorium with a resident nurse and doctor, the enlargement of the Upper Quadrangle and two new Houses. Economic conditions in the 1920s reduced entries from clerical and other professional families, but he renewed his improvements, which included the building of private houses for married masters. Sporting fixtures were extended, and academic standards rose. When he retired in 1925, it had 350 boys and had established itself among the older public schools.

By 1934, however, industrial depression brought numbers down to 298; and the Second World War placed it in a very difficult situation. From 1940 it was evacuated to a scattered group of country houses in Shropshire, while its buildings were a naval training establishment. Cadets manoeuvred on the sports fields on grey-painted ice-cream tricycles fitted with a short mast and compass for navigation and signalling exercises.

On returning to Lancing in 1945, it faced formidable difficulties, but recovery under Frank Doherty (Headmaster 1934–53) was remarkable. By 1948 numbers had doubled. A man of deep religious commitment, he made the Eucharist the chief Sunday service and was determined that education was based upon religion, while he also liberalized and humanized its ethos.

His successors John Dancy (1953–61), William Gladstone (1961–9), Ian Beer (1969–81) and J. S. Woodhouse (from 1981) have taken the College successfully through the post-war educational and religious problems. It now has 470 boarders and 26 day boys, while the VI Form has about 200 boys and 75 girls. Girls were admitted in 1970 when a local girls' school closed its VI Form, and they now reside in their own two Houses.

New buildings include technological and arts centres, a new swimming pool (1975), the sports hall (1982) and the theatre (1984). A computer centre was established within the science block in 1985, and all pupils follow a computer

course. Each pupil chooses a member of the teaching staff to be his own tutor, who helps him in his work and progress. Younger boys sleep in individual cubicles in dormitories and work in houserooms, where each has his own 'alley' with desk and bookshelves. Older boys have 'pitts', shared or individual studies. While the main team games are still important, there is now a greater variety, and sports options include badminton, aerobics, squash and windsurfing.

The whole College attends chapel every Sunday and on Saints' Days, and there is a daily celebration of Holy Communion. Every other year the 'Lancing Lecture' is given by a distinguished speaker on important world problems. In 1978 the chapel was completed with the building of the west front with its magnificent rose window containing the arms of the Woodard schools. The Prince of Wales attended the dedication, together with representatives of all the schools in this 'central minster' of the Corporation.

# Hurstpierpoint College

## SUSSEX

Founded as St John's School, a 'middle school', on 16 August 1849, the College was Woodard's earliest 'middle school'. It was situated in several houses in Star Lane, Shoreham, but moved from these cramped quarters on 29 January 1850 to the Mansion House and other places in Hurstpierpoint. He chose a site of 100 acres two miles from the village for its present buildings. These consisted of two quadrangles, designed by R. C. Carpenter and built in the local flint. The College occupied the first part of these buildings in 1853, which were finished in 1861 and· are the Corporation's first permanent buildings. R. H. Carpenter designed the chapel (1861), the infirmary, gymnasium and Headmaster's house. It stands on the first ridge of the Sussex Weald facing the South Downs and commanding a view of the whole range from Lewes to Chichester. John Keble said, 'It is a place to live and die in'. But the area was thought to hold undesirable temptations for the pupils. An early rule stated, 'No boys are allowed to go to Brighton without urgent cause'.

Its first Headmaster was the Rev. Dr E. C. Lowe, who had taught at St Nicolas School. He told the Taunton Com-

mission, 'We went into the school at a time when about a third of the buildings was a rough carcase, simply the walls and roof over, but unglazed, unfloored and unfurnished altogether'. Yet with fees at 33 guineas, it started well, having 72 pupils in 1850, 106 the next year and 217 by 1860. Lowe told the Taunton Commission that it attracted middle-class parents because 'they feel themselves to be childridden'. For those living in small houses with large families, it was an advantage for them to be able to delegate their authority and 'not to have their big boys always at home'.

The syllabus comprised the classics, English, French, geography, writing, book-keeping, vocal music, and mathematics. Boys who could not sing learnt physical science—only one musical boy wished to do both. Lowe

wanted to make the curriculum more up-to-date than Woodard would approve (see p. 7).

The boys' diet was quite substantial for the times. Breakfast and tea consisted of thick bread and butter (as much as could be eaten in half an hour) and half a pint of fresh milk and hot water; dinner was meat, bread and vegetables with half a pint of beer daily and pudding on four days a week. Prefects and captains had a supper of bread and cheese and beer. It was found to be cheaper to buy the meat in London than locally.

From 1857 to 1864 Sabine Baring-Gould taught there and wrote 'Onward Christian Soldiers'. He also designed the ironwork of the bookcases in the boys' library and painted the window jambs with scenes from the *Canterbury Tales* and the *Faerie Queen*.

When Lowe resigned in 1872 (see p. 000) there were 326 boys, sleeping in six dormitories. Besides the 'middle school', there were also three other sorts of pupils in the College. Until 1903 there were Probationary Associates aged from 17 to 20, 'promising boys with a vocation for training as Middle-Class Masters', who, after gaining a Certificate as an Associate of St Nicolas College, could study theology and seek ordination from a bishop. From 1854 to 1891 there were Servitors, local boys, who performed household tasks, such as cleaning boots and knives, sweeping and serving at table, and in return were taught for three hours in the evening by the Probationary Assistants; and from 1855 to 1874 there were boys studying technical and military subjects for the Indian Civil Service examinations.

It was a pioneering school. In April 1860 it was among the first six schools to have a cadet force. The *Hurst-Johnian* (with a cover designed by Baring-Gould) appeared in May 1858 and is the oldest school magazine. The Shakespeare Society, founded in 1854, has produced the longest series of annual productions of Shakespearian plays, interrupted only during this century's war years. Its choir, started in

 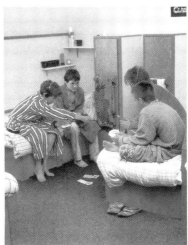

1854, is an early school choir; a school band was formed in 1861; and a school orchestra existed in 1859.

Three ceremonies started by Lowe survive. A service commemorates St Ethelreda's day (17 October), to whom the Chapel is dedicated, and since 1903 it has been Old Hurst-Johnian's Day. The Boar's Head Procession, derived from Queen's College, Oxford, takes place on the nearest Saturday to St Nicolas Day (6 December) when a boar's head is carried with lighted torches through the cloisters, followed by a 'stodge' (feast) for the choir; and on Ascension Day since 1850 the college has climbed nearby Wolstonbury Hill to sing a hymn and distribute Lowe's dole of money to the choir.

From 1890 to 1910 there was a College Bicycle Club, which early in the century rode to the rising buildings for Christ's Hospital, near Horsham. This school's removal to Sussex affected the college. Boys could go there with scholarships from the London County Council. By 1906 numbers were down to 118. They remained low until the First World War, when they rose to 218 by 1918.

The Rev. H. B. Tower (Headmaster 1924–7) was able to take advantage of this recovery. He was determined to

31

improve the reputation of the school and prepared to spend the money needed to do this. The inner buildings were finished, the long dormitories, extending the full length of the main buildings, were divided into cubicles in 1927, and a Junior School was established in 1933 (see p. 34). And in 1927 the construction of the tower completed the chapel, making the college the first Woodard school to have its planned buildings finished. By 1927 there were 267 pupils, including 12 day boys; but his expenditure had left only £6 in the bank, and no further major building was possible for twenty years.

During the 1930s the college organized 'Contact' to promote understanding with boys in the northern distressed areas. Pairs of boys of similar age, hobbies and tastes wrote to each other, and members of 'Contact' first met in 1936 when 20 boys from South Shields spent a weekend at the college.

Though the Air Ministry considered at one time using the site as an aerodrome, which would have meant cutting down trees and lowering the chapel tower, the threat came to nothing, and the college kept its buildings during the Second World War, when numbers and academic standards rose, so that a great post-war building programme was possible, making better provision for art, dramatics, music and science, and yet preserved the college's advantage of being a convenient and unified campus with everything, including sports fields, easily accessible. The seven Houses each have about fifty or sixty boys, divided between the years. Houses support a charitable cause of their own choice, and volunteers go to help the Burgess Hill Disabled Housing Trust.

The academic programme seeks to permit all pupils to study the maximum number of subjects up to the level of the GCSE, and some of the main subjects have been introduced at the new AS Level or GCSE (mature) Level. The 'Challenge of Industry' course is followed, and VI Formers are able to undertake a week's executive shadowing

with senior company executives. Besides the main team games, there is a wide variety of indoor sports: basketball, gymnastics, badminton and others.

There are about 360 boarders and 60 day boys and about 150 in the VI Form. It has been called a 'small school on a compact site with a strong sense of community and belonging'; and the present Headmaster has said that the changes and improvements have made it possible to give full expression to 'the humanity of the place and the range of choice available in all areas of school life'.

# *Hurstpierpoint College Junior School*

## SUSSEX

Dr Lowe told the Taunton Commission (1868), 'Within the last 18 months we have induced a lady to open a preparatory school for little boys about 2 miles from us. My hope is that by means of this school we should after a time have no boys coming to us under nine years old, who have not at that age entered at least upon the rudiments of learning'. No more is known of this school, which apparently did not last long; and nothing was done again until 1933 when the Rev. H. B. Tower, disliking boys aged 8 to 18 being placed indiscriminately in the dormitories and yet wishing to have young boys available for the college at the age of 13, began a Junior House with four boys and eight more the next year. As they were housed at the top of the Star Tower he called them 'Starlings.' But falling numbers (only two boys came in 1937) led to its closure in 1938.

It was revived in 1941 with 17 boys and 1948 given its own buildings by being transferred to the old sanatorium,

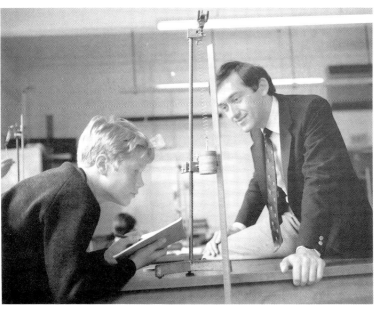

and there have been later extensions, including a library (1975) and science laboratories (1986). It also shares several of the college's facilities such as the dining hall, swimming pool and sports hall.

It became more independent in 1965 as Hurstpierpoint College Junior School. Most of its boys still proceed to the college, but a few now go to other schools. Under K. J. Heslop (Master 1954–72) numbers rose from 70 to 170. It now has 52 boarders and 106 day boys, a proportion which has been increasing in recent years. As well as the normal curriculum, boys take part in at least two weekly 'activities', ranging from stamps and modelling to drama and orchestra; and at the end of their last term they take part in the 'Leavers' Challenge', a walk in four stages along the South Downs Way to Bexhill.

# *Ardingly College*

## SUSSEX

Woodard said of the college, which he founded as St Saviour's School on 12 April 1858, 'It is the most precious jewel in our whole scheme'. It was a 'lower school', which occupied the buildings at Shoreham vacated by the 'upper school', when it went to Lancing. The Rev. F. M. D. Mertens, its first Headmaster (1858–94), had taught at Lancing. Woodard secured a site for it in 1862, near the village of Ardingly. The new buildings, designed by R. H. Carpenter, were begun in 1864 and the southern wings of the two red-brick courtyards opened in 1870; the northern wings were built in 1880 and 1927. The chapel, described by Pevsner as 'a noble piece for a school chapel', was built in 1883. It is on a hillside with a fine view into the valley of the river Ouse and the railway viaduct from the Terrace. The original plan was that it should be approached by a drive along the east side of the buildings, but this was thought to be too steep for middle-class parents' one-horse carriages.

At Shoreham it had 114 boys. Woodard wanted it to have 1,000 at Ardingly, and Gladstone called it 'Mr Woodard's *Great Eastern*'. It had also Probationary Assistants and Servitors from 1860 to 1895 (see p. 30), making it three schools in one; but its first buildings were only for about 400, except for the dining hall and kitchens, which were for the full number. It did not achieve this, but by 1871 there were 350 and 420 in 1886, being helped by fees of only 15 guineas—'little exceeding the cost of food'—(see p. 73) and the devotion of old boys on the staff.

The present dining hall was the temporary chapel, and classes were also taught together in it. Faces were slapped for bad marks in a lesson, and even VI Formers did their sums on slates. The subjects taught were reading, writing, arithmetic, vocal music, English and Latin grammar, book-keeping, drawing and history; French was ten shillings a quarter extra.

Football matches took place on the Hard with 40–50 a side, including masters. Association football was also played with other schools, but differences in rules caused

difficulties. On one day in 1874 an association match was played against Hurstpierpoint, followed by a rugby match. The College adopted rugby football in 1920.

Everyday life was hard. Open coal fires were not replaced by hot water pipes until 1875; and small, single-wick paraffin lamps (one in a day room, three in a dormitory) provided light. Along the muddy pathway between the two detached wings boys carried hot water from the kitchens to the dormitories every night. When taps froze in the winter and wells dried up in the summer, they were sent with buckets to streams in the surrounding woods. A table with two bowls at one end of every dormitory provided washing facilities, and each boy's trunk, kept beside his bed, was the only place for his clothes. There was little money for improvements.

Nevertheless changes were made essential by competition from the new secondary schools founded after the Education Act of 1902. No longer could it be a 'third-grade school', with simpler curriculum and absence of advanced work. The twentieth century's first two Headmasters, the Rev. H. A. Rhodes (1904–11) and the Rev. Marchant Pearson (1911–14), made the initial reforms. Science was started in 1906 with £15 worth of chemicals and apparatus in a disused dormitory. Greek was added to Latin, which became an alternative to German. Boys were encouraged to enter the VI Form instead of going to Hurstpierpoint or Lancing. The prefect system was developed, and masters ceased to play in inter-school cricket and football matches. In 1912 acetylene lighting was introduced; and a Junior House was founded (see p. 43).

Food shortage in the First World War reduced the boys' breakfast and tea to 'chunks and hoggy' (bread, margarine, and tea). The college was full during those years with 350 pupils, but post-war conditions reduced them to 186 by 1933, and its debts increased. Again shortage of money made improvements difficult. The first science laboratory was a wooden hut bought by selling Rivers Wood, and until the classroom wing, started in 1913, could be finished in 1927, boys still spent both lessons and leisure in rooms filled with desks, tuck boxes, overcoats, and boots.

The Rev. E. C. Crosse (Headmaster 1933–46) at once reduced the fees, which had risen from £40 in 1914 to £100, to 80 guineas. This and improving economic conditions turned the tide. By 1939 there were 333 boys. New buildings included the library and science school; and the Archway, with a VI Form room above, joined chapel and dining hall. Electricity was installed in 1939, just before war made carbide, needed for the acetelyne system, unobtainable.

In 1940 Crosse decided the college would remain where it was, but assured parents that he had 'arranged for every boy to have a bicycle or other means of getting home', before the buildings were captured by enemy invaders. German bombers were nightly heard passing over, and the fires burning in London lit the sky. The building suffered only broken windows from flying-bombs, when glass splinters had to be taken from desks before lessons. Basins and showers were ripped out of changing rooms, which became semi-underground dormitories lit by blue lights; here the boys slept every night in double tiers of bunks. Boys formed a Land Army, which grew most of the vegetables the school needed. HMS *Sluna*, a mine-sweeping trawler, was adopted by the college, which sent it comforts, including 1000 cigarettes a time, and received the ship's bell when it was scrapped in 1953. On VE Day the blackout (which had cost £100 to cover the Gothic windows) was burnt in a ceremonial bonfire. For the boys the war meant the end of wearing stiff collars on Sundays.

By 1945 numbers were 375, the maximum possible, and the VI Form had risen from five in 1933 to 57. Freedom from debt allowed post-war expansion. The Rev. George Snow (Headmaster 1946–61) introduced the present House system; individual 'study periods' supplemented 'teaching periods' in the timetable; and every boy had a

tutor to care for him pastorally and supervise his work. Unprecedented new building came with C. H. Bulteel (Headmaster 1962–80), particularly the music school, art school and technology centre.

Day boys were admitted in 1976. Girls entered the VI Form in 1972 and the rest of the School ten years later. Three-quarters of the 475 pupils are boarders, including 90 girls in a new boarding house built in 1988. The VI Form has 206, including 81 girls. Since 1978 the Upper VI house accommodates 96 pupils in study-bedrooms, boys at one end, girls at the other and an academic and social centre between.

The academic standard is high, and most pupils go on to higher education, but narrowness is avoided by taking general studies as well. The GCSE years take Religious studies and Learning for Living, a course on personal and social responsibility. The VI Form takes Religious Studies and a General Course on practical, contempory and intellectual subjects. Many trips are organized abroad, including exchanges with schools in Toulouse and Heidelberg. The school's declared aim is 'to enable all boys and girls to develop their love of learning, academic potential, and individual talents in a caring community, which fosters sensitivity, confidence, a sense of service, and enthusiasm for life'.

# *Ardingly College Junior School*

Woodard intended that St Saviour's School should have a 'petty school' with its own chapel and hall, dormitories and classrooms in the North School, but this was not achieved until 1912, when Marchant Pearson, wishing to house the younger pupils on their own, closed North School as a separate wing and transferred the 91 boys of the four lowest forms to a junior House there. It started well under J. G. Nicholson (Master 1912–28), who introduced Scouts (now joined by Guides) and monitors to help in the school. Though numbers fell in the 1930s to about 70, by 1937 they were over 100 and during the war rose to 120.

In 1949 it became Ardingly College Junior School, but most of its pupils still go on to the college. Day boys were admitted in 1967 and girls in 1986. Over half of its 200 pupils (including 80 girls) are now day pupils. New buildings include a technology department based in the old farm buildings and a science laboratory (1989); but chapel, dining hall, gymnasium and other facilities are shared with the college. This has meant in music, for instance, that a pupil may learn to play any instrument.

It has always been a school of varied activities. In 1944, for instance, after the Arnhem landings, it had a sale which raised nearly £74 for the Airborne Forces Security Fund. In 1974 it founded the Bacon and Lamb Essay Reading Society, which has meetings for pupils to read their own compositions in a darkened room. Similarly it seeks to encourage children, whose prowess is in academic studies, creative arts or athletics. For all it provides a Christian based community in which they can achieve their full potential.

# Bloxham School

## OXFORDSHIRE

In 1852 Woodard dismissed for 'flagrant insubordination' one of his Shoreham schoolmasters, John William Hewett. He became a curate at Bloxham, where he founded in 1855 All Saints' Grammar School, 'for the liberal education of the sons of the clergy, naval, military, professional men, and others', in a farmhouse, part of which remains as the core of the present school. He commissioned the prominent architect, George Edward Street, to produce elaborate plans for buildings around a quadrangle and a chapel, but only one wing, part of the north block, was finished when it failed within two years. Woodard refused an offer to buy it for £5,000, but in 1859 Reginald Egerton, a young Fellow of New College, Oxford, and curate at Deddington, near Bloxham, seeing the derelict buildings while on a walk, bought them for £1,500, which was all that he had.

Though his Fellowship of £200 a year was his sole income, he opened the school in January 1860 with one day-boy and an elderly housekeeper. A fortnight later, he liked to relate, he had twice as many pupils. In April he gained three boarders and two more day boys. By the end of 1860 there were 14 boys, 29 by November 1861 and 50 early in 1863. The prospectus for 1865 declared, 'Every boy has a single bed'. It made a pioneering move in 1865 in taking the Cambridge Local Examinations and becoming a 'Local Centre.'

The school could contain only 60 boys until he added new buildings with the generous support of his cousin, Harriet Gould, whom he married in 1862, and her family. He employed Street until the architect died in 1881, but his original plan was not followed, and the buildings, which cost nearly £30,000, were added piecemeal. Among these were the Schoolroom Wing with a dormitory above (1864), the dining hall (1869) and the chapel (1876). They brought the accommodation up to 200, but it was rarely above 100 during the next 20 years.

Egerton was a Tractarian and wished his private school to survive him with its religious character unchanged; therefore in 1884 he established it as a permanent foundation by vesting its property in trustees. Two years later he retired, but remained there as Warden until 1890, hindering the new Headmaster, the Rev. F. S. Boissier, who faced fresh problems. From 1870 parents were attracted by the cheap, new Board Schools, some of which introduced a new top standard in 1882; and by the late 1890s higher-grade schools provided technical, scientific or commercial secondary education. Moreover, agricultural depression struck local farmers and businessmen.

Boissier believed that the best future for the school lay in it becoming a Woodard school. In 1896 he persuaded the Corporation to accept the school from the trustees, though Woodard himself had thrice declined such an offer. He then loyally resigned, and the Rev. G. H. Ward (Headmaster 1898–1914) was appointed by the Corporation, which gave financial help to provide new buildings required by the times, notably a chemistry laboratory and gymnasium. Academic standards improved, and numbers, which had fallen steadily to 62 by 1900, rose to 104 in 1911.

This continued beyond the First World War, and V. L. Armitage (Headmaster 1925–40) set out with a new young

### GRAMMAR SCHOOL, BLOXHAM,

##### NEAR BANBURY.

THE School Buildings at Bloxham having been purchafed by the Rev. P. R. EGERTON, B.C.L., Fellow of New College, Oxford, will be opened by him (D. V.) on January the 31ft, 1860, as a Grammar School, for the education of the Sons of Tradefmen, Farmers, Clerks, and others of the Middle Claffes.

Bloxham is fituated within an eafy diftance of Banbury, where there are Stations of both the Great Weftern and North Weftern Lines.

The courfe of Inftruction includes the Englifh, French, and Latin Languages; Vocal Mufic; Writing, Arithmetic, and the other details of a found commercial education.

The Terms for Boarders are £25. 4s. per annum. Day Boys £6. 6s. per annum. Entrance fee for boarders £1. 1s., for Day Boys 10s. 6d. Thefe charges include every ex-penfe, except tradefmen's bills, books, and ftationery.

The Payments muft be made quarterly, in advance, one week before January 31, March 31, July 31, September 30, either to "The Bloxham School Account," at the Old Bank, Oxford; or to the Head Mafter.

The Head Mafter can receive a few boys into his own houfe at 30 guineas per annum. Greek, German, the Piano, and Drawing are extras.

A Quarter's dues, or Three Months' Notice, is required before removal of a pupil.

For further particulars apply to the Rev. P. R. EGERTON, Bloxham.

ABOVE *The first School Prospectus*

TOP RIGHT *The Rev. P. R. Egerton, about 1870*

RIGHT *One of the first boarders*

BELOW *The Schoolroom, 1864*

47

staff to achieve the necessary success in education and sport. By the mid-1930s about a third of the leavers went to the universities. Then he turned to its inadequate, old-fashioned, overcrowded premises, embarking upon a building programme which rivalled Egerton's. The untidy and somewhat ragged set of old buildings yielded to fresh, clean additions, faced in the local stone, such as the great hall and classroom block.

Despite this, however, economic depression again affected the school. Numbers fell from over 140 in 1936 to 120 in the summer of 1939. His principle of 'build now, pay later' had incurred a debt of some £14,000. Closure seemed likely.

The college was saved by K. T. Dewey (Headmaster 1940–52), who had been Second Master. He was able to take advantage of war-time conditions. Being in a safe area, the school gained pupils from the nearby bombed Midland cities, and it also attracted local farmers' sons. He increased the numbers still more by deliberately lowering the entrance requirements, both academically and in age. There were 200 pupils by 1942 (which was celebrated by a *Te Deum* in the chapel), and the debt was paid off in 1946.

The school seemed safe, but R. S. Thompson (Headmaster 1952–65) thought it poorly-equipped, old-fashioned and academically weak. By securing more laboratories, sports fields and improved accommodation for boys and staff, he prepared the way for the five-year plans of D. R. G. Seymour (Headmaster 1965–82), who first raised both academic and sporting standard so successfully that numbers increased from 250 to 320, requiring the building of the new Raymond House embodying the new idea of study-bedrooms. Much of his second five-year plan sought to widen the college's appeal and broaden its entry, which included admitting girls into the VI Form in 1974.

A Conference on Public School Religion, which he held at the school in 1967, produced the Bloxham Project to

consider the nature of a Christian school. Under successive directors it has inspired books and papers, discussion
groups and regular conferences at Bloxham for chaplains
and others concerned with religion in schools. The school
itself looks outwardly. Groups of pupils engage in local
public works, and through an organized community service programme in the neighbourhood over 100 weekly
visits are made to the elderly and handicapped.

Expansion from 1982 to 1986 brought a new sports centre, music school and technology centre. There are now
about 300 boarders and 70 day pupils; there are about 180
in the VI Form, a third being girls. The Headmaster's
Report in 1988 said, 'Our problem seems likely to be *not*
how to maintain numbers, but how to stop them increasing to the point where the nature of the school might be
changed. We shall remain a small school.'

# St Michael's School

## BURTON PARK, SUSSEX

'Public schools for girls are of very doubtful merit,' said Woodard. 'Religious homes or convents are more in harmony with my ideas'; but he had a friend, Miss Mary Anne Rooper, who in 1844 founded in Lansdowne Square, Hove, a boarding school with six girls, who were trained as maidservants. On attracting middle-class girls, it changed its character and moved to a larger house in Littlehampton.

When she died in 1855, Woodard helped her successor, Lady Caroline Eliot, to reorganize it. It became St Michael's School with her as its first Lady Warden, and she took its 30 pupils to an eighteenth-century mansion, Lennon House, in Bognor, which had 'a healthy climate suited to delicate children from abroad'. In imitation of the resident fellows of Woodard's schools, it had teaching 'canonesses', who governed it until it became a Woodard school in 1920. It was both a 'middle' and an 'upper school' with annual fees of 21 and 60 guineas respectively. The 'middle' pupils were daughters of 'the clergy, tradesmen and farmers and others of moderate means'; the 'upper' pupils, 18 'young ladies', were 'exclusively the

daughters of gentlemen', who ate and were taught with
the rest, but 'have a separate governess and schoolroom
and take their walks and amusements separately'. Each
had to bring a silver fork and spoon and six dinner
napkins. Corresponding to Servitors in boys' schools
were Industrials, girls (25 in 1868) aged from 10 to 13,
who did housework and were trained as maidservants.
They had 'no stated holidays, but a holiday can be
earned by good conduct'. Each was given distinctive
clothes, and 'when she is fitted for service, she will be
provided with a suitable wardrobe'. These divisions
were abandoned by Miss Frances Wheeler (Lady Warden
1886–94), who also added Latin, mathematics and science to the curriculum.

Miss M. G. Randall (Lady Warden 1895–1919), daughter
of a former Dean of Chichester, built a studio, laboratory,
museum and library in 1911. She made some weekday
changes, including summer sea-bathing from machines
before breakfast, but Sundays were unaltered. Veils were
worn in the chapel, the choir had its own common room,
and the girls repeated the collect of the day to her before

Morning Prayer. Afterwards they walked along the sea-front in a crocodile, wearing plain long black woollen cloaks and small round black bonnets with strings. During the First World War she introduced first-aid classes and lectures on aeroplanes, but when peace came, she disliked the staff wearing the newly-fashionable V-necked dresses. She was always clad in a black dress and mantle.

The inter-war years brought coach trips to Arundel, Goodwood and other places on Saints' Days, and the school was extended by the purchase of other nearby houses. Miss Batho (Lady Warden 1938–44) had to face the upheaval caused by the Second World War. Air raids caused the evacuation of its 150 pupils in 1940 to Penzance, where they occupied the Hotel Royale and Ponsandane House and used the School of St Clare's laboratories and sports fields. The bombing of Plymouth and inaccessibility of Cornwall caused its 45 pupils in 1942 to go to Heathfield School, Ascot, where they occupied the bedrooms of the 65 Heathfield girls' own servants, who had gone off on war-work; but both schools were taught together.

Before Miss Batho died, she arranged for the School to move permanently to Burton Park, a Georgian-style house (1842) with an estate of 150 acres below the Sussex Downs. Until Canadian troops relinquished this, its 70 pupils were

enabled by Lord Selborne to go to Blackmoor House, Liss, but on 27 September 1946 their entry into Burton Park was marked with a Eucharist in the ballroom, the temporary chapel. They survived the bitterly cold winter with classes in pantries, store-rooms and garages.

Since then, new buildings include the New Wing in which are the dining room and kitchen; a new classroom block and hall; a chapel; rooms for music, needlework, cookery, drama and art; and seven science laboratories. The school excels in music, drama, and sport and has produced 18 county representatives in lacrosse; it also plays the Sussex game of stoolball. There are some 200 boarders and 20 day girls. For their first year, girls live separately in Wakefield House, a converted eighteenth-century farmhouse, then in five Houses until they move in the VI Form to two separate houses, where they each have a study-bedroom and can do their own cooking.

The school joins with Lancing College in joint activities with the Archbishop Michael Ramsey School in Camberwell (see p. 58). It also co-operates with its neighbouring school, Seaford College; there is a joint Business Studies A-Level course, and boys have joined the Sixth Form cookery group.

The pupils worship in the school chapel and in nearby parish churches. The junior and senior choirs sometimes sing Evensong in Chichester Cathedral and local churches. The school is worthy of its declared aim to be a family unit based upon Christian life and teaching.

# The Archbishop
# Michael Ramsey School

## LONDON

London after the Restoration of the monarchy in 1660 was a pleasure-loving, extravagent city, but there was another side to it in the shape of the poverty-stricken slums where destitution and violence were rife. This situation inspired pious, generous-minded people to establish during those years a growing number of charity schools designed to provide the children of the poor with religious instruction and elementary education. One of the first of these bene-factors was Richard Lawrence, who in 1661 bequeathed the 'Dog House Fields' to establish a charity school, called the Lambeth Free School, for 20 poor children of Lambeth Marsh. The Archbishop of Canterbury became its patron, and in 1805 Archbishop Manners Sutton preached a charity sermon for the school, which 'succeeded in draw-ing £62 16 9d from the pockets of the congregation'. When the London and South Western Railway bought its site in 1899, it was rebuilt near Lambeth Palace and renamed Archbishop Temple's Boys' School. In 1961 it amalga-

mated with Archbishop Tenison's Girls' School, also founded as a charity school in 1696, and subsequently absorbed the parish schools of St Mary Newington and of St John and All Saints'. In the 1960s Southwark Diocese planned a new large comprehensive school in Camberwell on the site of St Michael and All Angels' School, a parish school built in 1903, bombed in 1944 and rebuilt in 1954. This merged with Archbishop Temple's School in 1974 to form the Archbishop Michael Ramsey School, a voluntary aided comprehensive Church school which now has 509 boys and 324 girls.

It consists of a series of purpose-built, low-level interlinked buildings with two playgrounds and two courtyard places, and the site is planted with flowers, shrubs, and trees. Here also was the wooden St Michael and All Angels' Church, which was closed in 1954 and replaced by a brick building that is both a parish church and a worship centre for the school, which uses it for drama and worship. The chaplain is shared by school and church. In 1978 the school joined the Oval Church Schools VI Form

Consortium of Archbiship Tenison's Grammar School and the Charles Edward Brooke School, establishing a single, integrated VI Form with a wide range of courses.

The Lancing College Mission, founded in 1909 (see p. 23), was connected with the church here, so it was appropriate for the college to be linked to the school, which was associated with the Woodard Corporation in 1981. A master of the College is a governor of the school. Sixth

of both schools and of St Michael's School, Burton Park, attend annual social studies classes and meet the problems of both the Inner City and prosperous Sussex. It is a union of schools which, in different circumstances, offer their pupils an education inspired by Christian ideals and in a religious environment.

Charity Boy
*drawn by Cheryl Allman*
*from a statue*
*at the school.*

# The Midland Division

From the early 1850s Woodard wished to extend his activities northwards, but for ten years he was engaged entirely in Sussex. Then Sir Percival Heywood, a landowner in Denstone, who had lost a son, was inspired when worshipping on All Saints' Day 1866 in the parish church to join with Henry Meynell, the vicar, to found a Woodard school there. With the support of John Lonsdale and George Augustus Selwyn, successive bishops of Lichfield, a Midland Division was now possible.

Woodard realized, like John Wesley in the previous century, the need for local organization and institutions to sustain local concern and enthusiasm. He had meanwhile arranged to 'deliver statutes' to a Chapter of Fellows in the Midlands for another division within the Corporation with the same autonomy as the South. This was constituted on 28 July 1873 as the Society of SS Mary and John of Lichfield at Denstone College, its central buildings.

He appointed a close friend as its Provost, Dr Lowe (see p. 27). As he was still concerned with his southern schools and was now also a canon of Manchester, he left the new Division largely to Lowe, whose ideas were more advanced than his own. In 1884 he opened St Augustine's Grammar School at Dewsbury, the only day school founded by the Corporation, but after an early success, it closed in 1899.

Lowe was more successful with girls' education, in which he was influenced by his sisters, who had a small girls' boarding-school in Middlesex. While still at Hurstpierpoint, he wrote a pamphlet, *Middle Class Boarding Schools for Girls in the Midland Counties.* Though Woodard was doubtful, his Midlands supporters wanted such a school as early as 1867. When he became Provost, he was helped by Meynell, Heywood, and other friends to buy a property in Abbots Bromley, where his brother, John Manley Lowe, was vicar. The opening there of St Anne's School (1874) and St Mary's School (1880) made the Division the pioneer of this extension of the Corporation's work. In 1887 it took over another girls' school, St Winifred's, Bangor, which moved to Llanfairfechan in 1922, but was closed in 1968. The Chapter decided in 1892 that 'the management of each school should be under the control of ladies, whilst the governing body should consist of the Provost and Fellows'.

Despite the difficulties of the school at Dewsbury, Lowe resolved to extend the Division. Ellesmere College was opened in 1884, and in 1890 the Duke of Newcastle gave a site for Worksop College. The next year Lowe became Provost of Lancing on Woodard's death. He was succeeded by Meynell, who secured its opening in 1895 the year when he went on to the Western Division.

Under his successors, the Division upheld its position. The Chapter noted in 1912 that under the Liberal government 'subscriptions continued to progress in spite of the increasing difficulty of collecting contributions under the present political regime'. During this century it gained three preparatory schools—Smallwood Manor (1922), Prestfelde (1929) and Ranby House (1948)—and St Hilary's School (1955). Its associated schools are Derby High School for Girls, the Bishop of Hereford's Bluecoat School (1983) and St Elphin's School (1987).

The Division has a full-time Provost and full-time Bursar. It is managed by the Standing Committee under the Provost's leadership with the support of the Divisional Bursar. The Chapter usually meets twice a year. Heads of schools do not attend the Standing Committee or, normally, the Chapter.

# *Denstone College*

## STAFFORDSHIRE

For a 'middle school', Sir Percival Heywood gave Moss Moor (together with £1,000), a farm of 50 acres, long a centre for cock-fighting, situated in the heart of the valleys of the Churnet and the Dove, close to the wooded vales of Alton. In 1867 a local paper condemned the 'Denstone College scheme for turning out a hundred Puseyite children every year'; but the next year St Chad's School was founded as 'a Public Boarding School for the commercial and agricultural classes of the Midland Counties'. In 1872 a vast garden-party at Alton Towers raised £5,000 for it, and Lord Shrewsbury gave its Big Schoolroom. It opened in 1873 with accommodation for 200 boys, which was soon increased to 400, but its numbers did not approach that. They were 46 at the start, rising to 100 in 1874 and 245 in 1890, including five Probationary Associates as at Hurst-pierpoint (see p. 30).

The buildings of grey Hollington stone, arranged around two open quadrangles (named after Bishops Lonsdale and Selwyn), were completed by 1878, except for the chapel and dining hall. The chapel was dedicated in

1887, a collection at the service realizing £1,500, which liquidated the debt on it; and the dining hall was finished in 1891. To Pevsner, 'The site is fine, the composition is sweeping and has never been destroyed'.

Lowe at first managed the school with four masters, four prefects chosen from the tallest boys, and four classes, the first and largest containing boys ignorant of Latin. The fees were 34 guineas a year. Conditions were hard. The first Headmaster, the Rev. W. B. Stanford (1875–9), retired with rheumatic fever. After several months the classrooms were finished. They served also as common rooms with rows of tuck-boxes, into which on one day a class placed alarum clocks that went off together during a lesson. The temporary chapel was arranged in a corridor, freezing in the winter and stifling in the summer. The SPCK gave 30 books, which were stored in a cupboard

until the library was built in 1881. Cricketers had to roll the pitches before and after practice and matches.

The Rev. David Edwardes (Headmaster 1879–1903) was thanked by the Division for his recognition of the 'modern requirements of science and of mercantile life'. New buildings included a cricket pavilion (1897) and a laboratory and gymnasium (1901), and the cadet corps was founded in 1900. His successor, the Rev. J. L. Dove (1903–05), made a pioneering move in putting the school clocks back half-an-hour between February and November.

Numbers remained so small that its future was doubtful, until the First World War, when the school increased so fast that by 1917 there were 314 boys, though the buildings were suitable for only 288. The dining hall (where bread and margarine replaced meat at dinner twice a week) could only contain everyone by removing the doors. During the winter of 1918 the dormitories were full of boys with influenza, who were sent home when they recovered, so that few were left to greet the Armistice.

Afterwards economic conditions and low fees hindered its expansion, though a block of 12 classrooms was opened in 1926. During the Second World War the college faced a continual threat of being requisitioned as an emergency hospital, and some playing fields were ploughed up to grow vegetables.

Dr B. M. W. Trapnell (Headmaster 1957–68) found that there had been little change for 40 years. He began a fund-raising drive for laboratories, playing fields, houses for married staff, a new hall, a heated indoor swimming pool, prefects' common room and VI Form studies; and in 1977 came the Centenary Building for art, metalwork, woodwork and drama.

Meanwhile day pupils, both boys and girls, had been admitted in 1976, and in 1981 the first of two boarding houses for girls was opened. The day pupils are attached to the six original Houses, as also are the girl boarders, though living separately. There are about 260 boarders and 100 day pupils. Since 1977 pupils have been admitted from the age of 11. The Houses in turn undertake the chapel services, to which parents of day pupils are invited.

For a comparatively small school it sends a good proportion of its pupils to university (some 25 a year). It seeks to encourage pupils to develop their individual talents, to the extent of awarding scholarships to any who contribute especially to the life of the school. Games have always been important with an emphasis on cross-country running and rugby, with the First XV as Staffordshire champions for the last two years; but now a greater variety includes fives, squash, tennis, and hockey (for the girls). Other activities include skiing trips and an expedition to Inaccessible Island. In 1988 the college took the first three places in the Midland Division's Talbot Prize for scientific projects.

# *Smallwood Manor School*

## STAFFORDSHIRE

In 1902 a preparatory school was founded at Denstone for boys aged from 7 to 13. They wore dark grey tweed or navy blue serge suits and Eton suits and black ties on Sundays. To gain larger buildings it moved in 1938 to Smallwood Manor, a country manor house built in 1886 and designed by Robert Edis, and was amalgamated with the existing Smallwood Manor Preparatory School. The house, which was unusually early in having electricity from the start, is in a wooded park of 60 acres two miles from Uttoxeter, nine miles from Denstone and seven from Abbots Bromley. Additions include an open-air heated swimming pool (1960), gymnasium/assembly hall (1965), music school (1970) and chapel (1979). Pupils also worship in Massingham Woodlands Parish Church, close to the grounds.

It now has some 60 boarders and 60 day boys and girls. Since 1984 there has been a pre-preparatory department for boys and girls aged three to eight, who get to know the main school by sharing some chapel services, lunching with it and using the library. Every pupil has a tutor, who is concerned with the child's academic and general progress. There is special provision for a few pupils with

65

dyslexia or learning problems. It is a separate community, but governed by the same Council as Denstone and on occasion uses the college's facilities.

It also has excellent facilities itself: two laboratories (it instituted a Preparatory Schools' Science Competition), a computer room, language laboratory, and art and handicraft rooms. The chapel choir sings regularly in Lichfield and Bristol Cathedrals, and most pupils learn to play a musical instrument. With 23 acres of playing fields, it has a strong sporting record, especially in rugby: the First XV won the Staffordshire Under 13 Cup in 1983, 1984 and 1987. There is an annual Expedition Day, a skiing trip during the Christmas holidays and a Lake District holiday in the summer.

# School of St Mary and St Anne

## ABBOTS BROMLEY, STAFFORDSHIRE

In 1872 Lowe established St Anne's School as an 'upper school' at Abbots Bromley, now a conservation village. He bought for it an impressive Georgian farmhouse with pan-elled rooms and broad tiled fireplaces, which, after adapta-tion, opened two years later with accommodation for 15 girls, though it began with nine. Its numbers, however, grew to 50 by 1878, 120 by 1905 and some 200 in 1922. Two houses with over 20 acres of extra ground were bought in 1904 and The Crofts, a fine country house with a pleasant garden, in 1917.

Miss Alice Mary Coleridge was its Lady Warden from 1878 to 1899. Refusing a salary and serving 'for love of God', she was responsible for the girls' spiritual and moral training and the Headmistress for their education and discipline. The post of Lady Warden lapsed in 1902.

During these early years, pupils rose at 6 a.m. and had three-quarters of an hour to dress before first lesson; dur-ing Lent there was an extra quarter of an hour's drill before breakfast. Everyone did writing exercises, and bad grammar meant a ½d fine for the Building Fund. A pupil said, 'The day seems an eternity, parents and home far away and unreal, only cold and loneliness and hunger are realities and grim ones'. The midday slice of currant bread was called 'brother' because one currant said to another, 'Brother, where art thou?' and the portions of fish served on Fridays were known as 'brown paper parcels.' The whole school assembled for 'characters' on Saturday mornings, when erring girls stood up and sadly recounted their misdeeds. On Saturday mornings too, each girl had four ounces of sweets when she had darned her black stockings properly. They went on 'walks, long walks, and on Saturdays, very long walks.' Every year there was a party for their parents and friends; the gentlemen had sugar, spiced wine and toast in the Library, the ladies pork pies, tea and bread and butter in a dormitory.

In 1880 Miss Coleridge opened across the village street St Mary's School, a 'lower school', to educate more cheaply 'the daughters of clergymen and other professional men of limited means and of the agricultural and commercial classes generally'. The teaching 'qualifies girls to become governesses or schoolmistresses', while 'at the same time, they are trained for the homely duties of life, to become good accountants and good needlewomen'. Besides several Industrials (see p. 52), who lived in outbuildings, it could accommodate 30 boarders. Starting with five girls, it had 38 by 1886 and 58 by 1890. Dr Lowe and Miss Coleridge raised funds for grants for clergy daughters; and the persevering, self-sacrificing efforts of Miss Agnes Gamlen (Headmistress 1890–1921) and her staff gained a large extension to the buildings in 1911.

Early life was austere. The first Headmistress was told to manage on 'the smallest possible budget'. Book-cupboards were adapted orange boxes, and the girls slept in open dormitories with long wooden washstands down the middle. Once a week their boots were cleaned, and each girl bathed in the laundry in a bucketful of water in a tin bath. Few parents could afford to keep their daughters

*St Anne's Chapel*

there beyond a year. A stay of two years was unusual,
and a few went on to St Anne's.

Gradually, however, the two schools grew alike, and from
1911 St Mary's was described simply as 'for daughters of
professional men and others'. Both always used the fine
Gothic St Anne's Chapel (built in 1881), though at separate
services and with different choirs. Both increased in numbers and buildings, until they joined to become the School
of St Mary and St Anne in 1921. St Anne's Guild, founded
in 1884, became the Guild of St Mary and St Anne, whose
members still 'set before themselves the highest standard

of Christian living'; and St Mary's clergy daughters' grants became about 100 'St Mary's Exhibitions'.

Since then the school buildings have developed on both sides of the street. St Anne's now includes the Junior School, the chapel, assembly hall, library, the music school and main teaching rooms with five laboratories and the art, computer and audio-visual centres. St Mary's has the sports hall with two squash courts, a heated indoor swimming pool and the medical centre.

The 1920s brought fresh changes. In 1925 girls could listen to the radio at 1d a time in the library, and the next year parents were allowed to visit their daughters in cars. In 1927 the Political and Social Problems Club debated 'That this house regrets the existence of fascism' (and in 1970 'That this house believes marriage is a dying institution'). For 40 years from about 1920 the school supported a mission to Longton, a poor parish in the Potteries.

During the Second World War, in the absence of air-raid shelters, the girls slept on palliasses in the corridors. The newly-formed Girls' Training Corps learnt first-aid and passive defence. Food rationing brought water-cress and dry bread for tea. Balaclava helmets and seaboot stockings were knitted and, when peace came, red pullovers for the children of liberated Europe.

Since then, as well as acquiring important new buildings, the school has grown and developed. It now has 300 girls including 60 day pupils and 72 VI formers, who have a choice of 24 A Level subjects in any combination. The latest addition to the curriculum is Business Studies and Information Technology. Its musical activity includes two choirs, an orchestra, a wind band, string ensembles and other chamber music groups. The Lower VI have study bedrooms and the Upper VI two special wings in St Anne's. There is a separate junior House for girls between seven and eleven and six senior Houses. The united school has not only responded to a new age, but also maintained its academic excellence, social training, and religious inspiration.

# Ellesmere College

## SHROPSHIRE

Woodard's wish for a 'lower school' in the Midlands was realized in 1877, when Lord Brownlow gave some 70 acres on his estate at Ellesmere for St Oswald's School, which the local press termed 'a great Jesuit plot to contaminate the backbone of England'. It was built H-shaped around two open quadrangles. It was planned that all pupils and staff live under one roof with a magnificent view from the terraces across the Shropshire Plain to the Breiddon Hills and the Berwyn Mountains beyond.

When it opened in 1884, half the planned buildings were finished, including dormitories for 100 boys and a dining hall for 400, but this was divided into two halves: one for meals, the other as a temporary Big School in which six classes were taught. Big School was built in 1894 and the Big School classrooms ten years later. Water came first from a well worked by two donkeys, and a horse and trap were kept to fetch goods from the town.

Big School was the day room for all boys, and members of 'Radiator Clubs' secured the warm places. In 1981 it gained from the disused church of St Mary, Tyne Dock, an internationally famous Schultze organ built in 1864.

Religious services were held in the covered playground beneath the dining hall until the chapel was built as a memorial to the boys of the Midland schools killed in the First World War, the first section being finished in 1928, the second in 1959. In 1966 fire destroyed the dining hall and chapel. Both were rebuilt, the dining hall with a lower flat roof.

The first Headmaster, the Rev. J. Bullock, was thanked on retirement in 1890 'for the public spirit and self-sacrifice displayed by him in making the playground'. He designed the conversion of the sloping grounds into terraces for playing-fields, which boys and staff began levelling in the first term, a task that was not finished until 1942. For many years the dormitories in turn rolled the cricket pitch. From the start rugby football was adopted, but matches were difficult because few other schools then played it. The college played also its own sort of football after breakfast with sometimes 100 participants. Association football

was adopted in 1904 (and also hockey), but in 1913 rugby was revived.

At first there were 81 boarders, but the next year '156 boarders and a few day boys—four beds only remain unfilled'. They came about equally from professional, business and farming families, and shorthand was introduced for their benefit in 1888. The fees were 18 guineas, 'little more than the cost of food' (see p. 38). At the end of the first term the Headmaster wished the boys 'a happy vacation in proportion to the energy with which each had worked'. For some 20 years the college had Probationary Assistants and Servitors (see p. 30). Its nearness to the great northern industrial towns was advantageous, but it depended also upon the countryside, and agricultural depression delayed the completion of the dormitories, and numbers were below 200 up to 1914.

During the war cricket and football were played with nearby military camps, but hockey was limited to inter-dormitory matches. The cadets paraded each morning and on Tuesday and Friday afternoons. The Cadet Corps had been founded in 1900 when its uniform was a dark blue Norfolk-shaped suit and a slouch hat. Numbers increased, reaching 246 in 1918, but then soon fell again.

The Rev. Dr A. V. Billen (Headmaster 1927–35) established the House system in place of the dormitories, which were two Reds, two Yellows, two Blues and two Violets. He also began the building of the chapel (but abolished pre-breakfast services) and brought the junior school (founded in 1921 in a house on St John's Hill in the town) to the college, where it stayed until 1960 (see p. 75).

The young, energetic Rev. R. A. ('Beef') Prosser (Headmaster 1935–61) resolved to overcome 'the opposition of the luxurious secondary schools built out of the rates', and prepare boys for medicine, engineering and other expanding professions. He gave bursaries for boys remaining at school to take the School Certificate, usually at 16. Despite financial constraints, he added 100 beds to the

dormitories, opened the science wing (1939) and made provision for music and art, hitherto taught in odd rooms and passages. After remaining low for 20 years, numbers rose, and the college's safe position in the Second World War brought them to over 300.

It now includes day boys, girls in the VI Form and a lower school with an entry at the age of 11. There are about 170 boarders and 80 day boys divided into 6 Houses, each with a study day room and recreation room, and 50 VI Form girls. During 1981 the arts centre for music and drama, the Nankivell VI Form Study Centre with 60 individual studies and a common room, and the creative design and technology centre were added to its buildings, which stand amid lawns, trees and gardens; and the main campus is surrounded by fields. In 1984 a boarding house was opened for the VI Form girls.

All pupils take a first-year broad foundation course and are guided in the GCSE course by a Personal Tutor, while VI Formers have an Academic Supervisor. The need for private study is stressed. There are several orchestras, the chapel choir is of cathedral standard, and two organ scholarships have recently been won. Outdoor pursuits include sailing on Whitemere, and since 1981 climbing and expeditions from its own field centre at Cwm Penmachno on the edge of the Snowdonia National Park.

# *Prestfelde School*

## SHREWSBURY

St Alban's Preparatory School was founded in Prestfelde House in 1929 by the Rev. G. Kendal Dovey with ten boys and his sister, Miss Edith Dovey, as matron and secretary. With increasing numbers, especially of boarders, Beckbury House (1931) and Highfield House (1946) and 27 acres of grounds were bought. The first chapel was in a loft over the Prestfelde House stables, but in 1936 a garden fête raised money to build St Alban's Chapel.

When it was acquired by the Woodard Corporation in 1949, the Rev. S. E. W. Young, the chaplain, became Headmaster. On becoming Ellesmere College's Junior School in 1960 (see p. 73), teaching was transferred to a new classroom block, and all three houses contained the increased number of boarders.

Michael Manby (Headmaster 1962–83) found that, while there were 50 boarders and 84 day boys, science was not taught, though 'a few bunsen burners' were bought in 1958, and the library had only 161 books in a classroom cupboard. He secured a steady increase in numbers, buildings and academic standards. The total of 200 boys was achieved (including 113 boarders) in 1972, and in 1980

a pre-preparatory department was started in new buildings. There is now also a nursery/reception class for three- and four-year-olds.

New buildings have culminated in the Edward Young Building (art and design centre) in 1986. Changes have ranged from carpeting in the dormitories to allotting less time in the timetable to Latin and more to science. In 1984 the chapel acquired a fine chamber organ, and its choir, together with the choral society and chamber choir express the importance of music in the school.

It has now about 100 boarders, 110 day boys and 60 children in the pre-preparatory department. Since 1978, instead of being Ellesmere College's Junior School, it has 'a special link with the college, but also takes boys destined for other schools'.

# *Worksop College*

## NOTTINGHAMSHIRE

In 1890 the Duke of Newcastle gave Lowe 150 acres (now 310) in the Clumber estate south of Worksop for St Cuthbert's School, another Midlands 'lower school', and laid out the roads and grounds. The drive to the School started opposite the gates of Welbeck Abbey, the Duke of Portland's seat. When the school opened in 1895, the buildings, designed by R. H. Carpenter in an imposing Queen Anne style, included a dining hall 132 feet long with an enormous hammer-beam roof copied from Westminster Hall. The Headmaster's house and the northern side of the quadrangle up to the clock-tower were built in 1897, the rest of the northern side in 1907 and the eastern side in 1928. The Gothic Chapel, designed by Aston Webb and given by Viscount Mountgarret (see p. 115), was completed in 1911.

It began with four masters and 25 boys, who within a year became 100. Latin was the basis of the curriculum for all pupils, except the Servitors (see p. 30), who competed for a Housework Prize. As well as new buildings, progress was marked by the fitting up of a science laboratory in the laundry in 1896, the gaining of the first university scholarship in 1902 and the introduction of the Cadet Corps in 1900 and Boy Scouts in 1909. From 1910 purple gowns were worn by the three senior prefects and blue ones by the rest.

During the First World War, when zeppelins approached, everyone went into the cellars, and to compensate for such disturbed nights the boys had an extra half-hour in bed each morning. Women temporarily joined the staff, including a young Latin teacher who married a prefect. On the outbreak of influenza in 1918, 170 fit boys were sent home, and some mothers came to help in nursing the remaining 43 and almost all the masters.

In 1925 the Board of Education reported scathingly on the school, stating that the examination results that year amounted to six School Certificates, and no university awards had been gained for 15 years. There were no studies for senior boys nor common rooms for the juniors, and hot water was available for most boys only once a week. Fortunately this was followed by the appointment of Canon F. J. Shirley, whom *The Times* was to call 'one of the most talked-about headmasters in modern Britain'. In a printed circular he expressed his wish to make it the 'Eton of the Midlands', and he transformed its fortunes by raising its academic level, developing its sport to secure it publicity, and improving its amenities. He changed its name to 'Worksop College', made the four dormitories into Houses and added two others. The school had changed in 1922 from association to rugby football, which he formally established; he also introduced hockey and himself umpired most of the matches, besides producing the annual Shakespeare play and taking the leading role himself. He harried the School Council and raised money

by loans and appeals. The climax to his building plans came in 1934 when he induced the Prime Minister, Ramsay MacDonald, to arrive by aeroplane to open the new laboratories and preparatory school. During his head-mastership, 13 university scholarships and 15 exhibitions were gained, and the average annual examination results were 60 School Certificates and 36 Higher Certificates. When he went to King's School, Canterbury, in 1935, he controversially took with him 3 masters and 22 boys.

During the Second World War, outdoor trenches were dug by the boys some 100 yards from the main school, one for each House, but these were never used. At first shelter again was taken in the cellars during air-raid warnings, but then reliance was placed upon firewatchers. Some 20 men from Poland and Eastern Europe helped in running the College.

From the 1950s rapid change and expansion took place. New buildings included the Winston Churchill Assembly Hall and Theatre (1974), the Northcote-Green Centre for craft, design and technical project work (1980) and a com-puter room (1983). Among changes were teas for visiting parents and a Parents' Liaison Committee, the develop-ment of 'horse-boxes' (study spaces) in the dormitories and the establishment of a VI Form Club, 'a licensed oasis for those of legal age for a brief period each evening'. In 1978 day girls were admitted and boarders in 1983.

There are now 275 boarders and 145 day pupils includ-ing 140 in the VI Form and 110 girls. There are six boys'

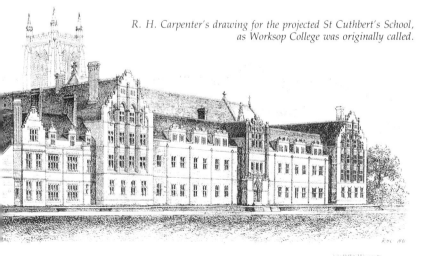

*R. H. Carpenter's drawing for the projected St Cuthbert's School, as Worksop College was originally called.*

boarding Houses all in the main school, and one for day girls and another for boarders, each in a nearby separate building. While it enjoys advantages from its grounds, its nearness to Worksop also enables pupils to participate in forms of community service, such as teaching in local primary schools, work in a remand home and helping the handicapped.

# *Ranby House School*

## NOTTINGHAMSHIRE

From about 1912 there was a preparatory school at Worksop for a few boys, mostly under 12 years old, supervised by the Matron. They had to march out morning and evening to wash in a changing room, and the theatre was their common room. It received new buildings in 1934, when it numbered about 90, its old quarters becoming the newly-formed Shirley House.

In 1948 the Corporation bought Ranby House, in the countryside north of Sherwood Forest and near Retford, with 30 acres of grounds, park and woodland, to be a preparatory school governed by the School Council of Worksop. It was originally the mansion of the Bingham family, who were wealthy Sheffield steelmasters. The house has a fine panelled hall with a huge central hearth, and one dormitory has panelling by the Yorkshire cabinet-maker, Robert Thompson, whose work always bears a carved mouse as his emblem.

At first there was accommodation for only 30 boys in

the house, so 60 remained at Worksop until the preparatory school there was closed in 1953. At Ranby the coach-
house and stables were converted into the chapel, and an
organ was installed in 1962. As new classrooms were constructed in the quadrangle, those in the house became
dormitories, and so more boys came. Other additions
were a sports pavilion, swimming pool, dining hall, new
chapel, gymnasium, resources centre and computer
department and science laboratories, and 15 acres of land
were made into sports pitches.

It now has some 90 boarders, boys and girls, and 115
day children, together with 45 in a nursery and pre-
preparatory department. Before coming to the School,
new pupils are invited to spend a day there, and at the
beginning of their first term they are helped by older boys
and girls as their 'guardians.' Special provision is made for
children with certain learning difficulties. Art and music
are strongly encouraged; nearly two-thirds of the pupils
learn to play a musical instrument; and a weekly hobbies
evening is run by parents and staff.

# St Hilary's School

## ALDERLEY EDGE, CHESHIRE

Alderley Edge High School for Girls was founded in 1876 by Miss J. Joyce, its first Principal, for the residential area stimulated by the opening of the railway to Manchester in 1842. It occupied a large Victorian house in the village's semi-rural outskirts and later gained two adjacent ones also. Miss Agnes Davis became Principal in 1913, renamed it St Hilary's School and did much to establish its reputation. She gave it a firm religious basis with unusually high academic standards and freedom for the girls. During the First World War its Girl Guides peeled potatoes and rolled bandages at a military hospital in a large house nearby, while other girls earned 2d for every plantain they dug up in the tennis courts.

Miss Davis was succeeded in 1927 by Miss H. C. Alcock and Miss D. M. Gliddon, as Joint Principals, who shared in the teaching and took daily prayers in turn week by week. The school experienced the inevitable shortages of books, paper and even desks in the Second World War, besides rationing, which reduced supper for resident staff and boarders to bread and cheese (and sometimes a baked potato), followed by bread and jam. Until the building of a kitchen and dining-room some years after the war, day girls had their lunch in two sittings in the Bluebird Cafe and the Corner House in the village.

In 1950 the Principals retired, appointed Miss E. Dawson as Headmistress (1950–60) and in 1955 transferred the school to the Woodard Corporation. It then had 229 day girls and 22 boarders. The girls became used to episcopal visitors, whom one called 'Prime Ministers in purple jerseys'. The Corporation, supported by the Parents' and Friends' Association, contributed liberally to its new buildings, among them three science laboratories (1974), an art studio (1977), the Centenary Sports Hall (1980) and a computer room (1982).

This was accompanied by a widening of the School's activities. Two important events in 1961 were the first annual Speech Day and the attendance of senior girls at the Worksop Ball (wearing short party frocks, ballerina length). Other annual events include ski trips abroad and exchanges with a Parisian school. The Junior School exchanged visits with the Elmslie Girls' School in Blackpool (see p. 129). In 1986 the school won first and second places in the Midland Division competition for teams of pupils undertaking scientific research. All girls learn to play a musical instrument.

There is a weekly service of Holy Communion in a small chapel built in 1975, a daily assembly in the hall and special services in the parish church. Entirely a day school

since 1974, it has 120 Junior pupils and 240 Seniors with 40 in the VI Form who since 1977 have a centre with common rooms, library and careers room. With small classes and a good staff–pupil ratio, it gives a broad education with the expectation that women may fulfil several roles in their professional and family lives.

# Derby High School

In 1870 two sisters, Mrs Elizabeth Coates and Miss Jane Cubley, and their half-sister, Miss Emily Coulson, founded a girls' school in Derby. It was so successful that within 20 years it moved twice, each time to a larger house. Its founders gave it an Evangelical tone and a remarkably wide curriculum for girls, including Latin, mathematics, French and history, but with the usual emphasis on drawing, painting and needlework. Bad work was punished by having to hem slate-cloths.

The Church Schools Company bought and renamed it Derby High School in 1892. The Company continued its pioneering character with the initiation of a botanical laboratory (1905) and hockey (1902) and cricket (1907). Numbers rose from 69 to 100 in 1903, but then it lost money. To prevent its closure, Spencer Noakes, archdeacon of Derby, formed a governing body, which bought it from the Company and reopened it with 30 girls.

During the First World War, when the girls grew vegetables which they sold to buy classroom cupboards, numbers grew to 155, and in 1920 Mrs Walter Evans of Darley Abbey bought for it Field House and Beechwood in Osmaston Road, where it had 215 pupils within a year; but in

1929 the economic crisis made it seem that it would become an aided school. A parents' meeting supported the governors' wish to preserve its independence and retain its junior school. The staff accepted lower salaries, and fees were raised. By 1939 numbers had risen to 149.

In 1939 its directed place of evacuation was Mackworth House, only two miles away. The Seniors were taught in the nearby Poplars farmhouse, but for a week in the spring term snow deprived them of all lessons. As numbers seriously declined, it returned to its own buildings at Easter. Two teachers firewatched nightly in turn in the school, enduring on clear nights black fumes from oil drums burning along the road to make protective artificial clouds. As girls could not go away, parents and teachers together provided games, visits, play-readings and other holiday activities, and the older girls worked in harvest camps each summer.

Miss L. M. Ogle (Headmistress 1939–50) led the school through the war and afterwards. In 1946, when it had 297 pupils, the first annual Garden Fête was held, and 1947 brought the formation of the Parent–Teacher Association. By then its buildings were clearly inadequate. Archdeacon

C. F. Richardson, helped by local industrialists, secured it a site on high ground on the city outskirts, where it moved into a new building in 1957. Miss Dorothy M. Hatch (Headmistress 1957–77) supervised this and made such innovations as the Tuesday Club discussion group and exchange visits to France, Germany and Switzerland.

The new site made possible further expansion, including more buildings and additional sports fields; and in 1980 Sutherland House and its grounds were bought for the kindergarten. There are 227 pupils (including 50 boys) in the kindergarten and junior school, 230 girls in the senior school and 38 in the VI Form. It became an associated Woodard school in 1958; it has a chaplain who conducts services and prepares pupils for confirmation. It maintains its reputation as a pioneering school with a strong Christian atmosphere.

# The Bishop of Hereford's Bluecoat School

## TUPSLEY, HEREFORD

The Bluecoat School in Hereford was one of a number of charity schools throughout the country named after the costume, often blue, worn by the children. Founded in 1710 to clothe and educate 40 boys and 30 girls, it was maintained by subscriptions and the collection at an annual charity sermon in the parish church. The boys wore a blue coat, leather breeches and knitted hose; the girls a blue dress, white apron, bonnet and tippet. In 1759 the mistress received half a guinea for candles used in cutting out the garments; and a barber was paid a guinea for 'cutting hair', which both boys and girls had cropped. The boys were taught to read and write, the girls to read only, and as late as 1827 'the propriety of teaching the girls to write was considered'. The girls were taught needlework and earned money for the school by undertaking embroidery for local ladies. In 1869 they 'finished some very beautiful work, part of a wedding order, which gave great satisfaction'. Though holidays coincided with the hop-harvest, two girls in 1821 were 'expelled the school for absenting themselves and going hop-picking'.

Richard Dawes, Dean of Hereford 1850–67 and a keen educationalist, improved the condition of the School, which soon attracted 'the children of the tradespeople', who were admitted after 1856 on the payment of moderate fees in addition to the free children; and in 1863 he brought about the introduction of a scheme of payments graduated according to the parents' means, while 70 free scholarships were still reserved for poorer children.

The twentieth century saw more changes. In 1921 it became entirely a girls' school, being designated a Senior School in 1932 and a Secondary Modern School in 1944. Numbers rose rapidly, and in 1958, when it took over the building of the High School for Girls, they reached 830. Also in 1958 the Bishop's School, a Church Secondary Modern School for boys and girls, was founded at Tupsley on the outskirts of the city; and in 1973 the Bluecoat School joined with this to form the Bishop of Hereford's Bluecoat School, a Church Voluntary Aided Comprehensive School with 1,100 boys and girls aged between 11 and 16. It became an associated Woodard school in 1983.

The extended building at Tupsley, which has 10 acres

of sports fields, was opened in 1977. There are four Houses—Ashley, Cheshire, Livingstone and Shaftesbury —and each meets daily for assembly and worship, has a service of Holy Communion every term and supports charities connected with its patron Christian reformer. Each has a Parents' Association, and at their request there is a termly parents' service. A classroom is used also as a school chapel.

The building is adapted with lifts and ramps for physically-handicapped children and has a special needs unit for 39 pupils. Three-quarters of the pupils go on to VI Form Colleges or other schools, and it has twice won the Midland Division science competition. Staff and pupils join in conferences and other activities with the Woodard-schools; and it holds an annual Christmas Concert and Carol Service in Hereford Cathedral. It well fulfils its declared aim that 'Christian principles should determine the way the school is organized and run'.

# St Elphin's School

## DARLEY DALE, DERBYSHIRE

In 1697 local clergymen founded the Warrington Institution, which met annually and took a collection for clergy
widows and adult orphan daughters in the Parish Church,
which is dedicated to St Elphin, a little-known saint who
died in battle in the seventh century. In 1844 it was
decided to help younger girls also, and the Rector of Warrington, Horace Powys, founded St Elphin's Church of
England School for the Daughters of Clergy (at first with
three pupils) in a vast, rambling former convent said to be
haunted by a nun. It shared this building and the chapel
with a Training College for Schoolmistresses (later St
Catherine's College, Liverpool). The girls called the college students 'Betties', who retaliated with 'clergy brats'.

The girls rose at six in the morning, when they had to
show that their stays were laced straight and their teeth
and nails were clean. The school year was not changed
from two halves to three terms (see p. 21) until 1880
because of doubts whether parents could afford to pay the
girls' extra train journeys. In the Big Schoolroom, four
classes were held at once, one in each corner, while the

92

Headmistress sat at a desk on a small platform at one end, occupied with her work, but ever ready to call out a misbehaving girl, who had to write her name and offence in a 'Black Book'. A common punishment was to darn stockings during recreation time, while a girl who stooped had to stand with a book on her head. The older girls played hockey wearing red blouses, red Tam o' Shanters and long navy skirts, but the young ones could only swing and bounce balls.

Miss C. L. Kennedy (Headmistress 1896–1910) ensured that an increasing number of girls went to universities. She also faced a crisis in the school's history. It had been founded in country surroundings, but now Warrington had become unhealthily industrialized; and in 1904 the drains were thought to have caused a severe outbreak of scarlet fever. The girls were sent home and taught by correspondence until the school moved with 68 pupils from Lancashire to Darley Dale, near Matlock in the Derbyshire moors, into a former hydropathic hotel standing in a wooded park of 51 acres and designed in an elegant late nineteenth-century Tudor style with a wood-panelled entrance-hall and a spiral staircase. A corrugated iron chapel was built; the altar end was curtained off when the Headmistress taught divinity, and the girls were told

'curtains, not hats'. Richmal Crompton (Miss R. C. Lamburn), author of the 'William' books, was a pupil (1901–11) and teacher (1914–17) at St Elphin's, but assured the school that her hero's exploits were not based upon her experiences there.

Under Miss M. L. Flood (Headmistress 1910–33) the school faced the difficulties of the First World War. Maize puddings, difficult to swallow, were served, but the situation was eased when a parent gave a barrel of glucose and another a cask of sugar. It joined the Patriotic Union of Girls' Schools and knitted socks and scarves in the tradition of those girls at Warrington, who had helped at soup kitchens during the Lancashire cotton famine of the 1860s. The stables (previously used as a gymnasium) were made into the chapel in 1916—and the girls were allowed to play table-tennis on Sundays. The next year secretarial subjects and personal health and hygiene were taught. Daughters of the laity were admitted as pupils from 1920. The Head Girl in 1926 presented a four-valve radio set to the school, which eagerly listened to the Savoy bands and to the news during the General Strike.

Miss M. Hudson (Headmistress 1933–41) faced serious financial difficulties and declining numbers. Partly by admitting day and weekly boarders in 1933, she turned a deficit into a substantial credit and raised numbers from 90 to 183.

The years after the Second World War saw much development and expansion, especially under Miss P. M. Robinson (Headmistress 1958–75). Miss Flood had introduced the idea of Houses, but only for the purpose of naming teams competing in games. Miss Robinson gave each House its own dormitory or cubicles, common room and house mistress. Girls became sacristans, servers and readers in the chapel. New buildings included single study-bedrooms for the Upper VI, three new teaching blocks, four science laboratories and specialist rooms, one being for computers (first introduced into the school in

1981). Since 1978 the girls have worn Douglas tartan kilts as part of their uniform.

The school has some 300 girls aged seven to eighteen, about half being boarders, and an Infants' Department for girls and boys aged three to seven. There is special tuition for dyslexic pupils. It has had a resident chaplain since 1962 and became an associated Woodard school in 1987. It is thus the latest school to enter into fellowship with the Corporation, but one that has always shared the aims and ideals of the founder.

# The Western Division

On acquiring King's College, Taunton, Woodard wrote, 'Here therefore we take our point of departure for constituting our centre for the West, and thus giving . . . the foundation of three out of five of our Educational Divisions for the entire Kingdom'; but for years the school, owing to its financial weakness, was controlled first by him and then by the Southern Division. Henry Meynell was largely responsible for the constitution of the Western Division as the Society of SS Mary and Andrew in 1897, when he came from the Midland Division to be the first Provost of Taunton. Its eight Fellows—five clerical and three lay—were supporters of King's College, which Woodard had intended as its central buildings. The Western Division took over the school, which reopened that year.

The Division now also owns the School of St Clare in Penzance (1928), Llandaff Cathedral School (1957), Grenville College, Bideford (1964) and St Margaret's School, Exeter, previously an associated school (1975). King's College Junior School, Pyrland Hall, and the Pre-preparatory School, King's House, were amalgamated in 1987 to form King's Hall.

Its three Chapter meetings each year are each residential over two days. The November meeting is at Taunton, while the two others are held at Bideford, Exeter, Cardiff, and Penzance in rotation. Heads attend and give an account of their schools, but are not present at sessions devoted to Chapter business. A Chapter Dinner, to which spouses and the local school's council and staff are invited, makes them both business and social occasions.

# King's College

## TAUNTON

In 1293 a free grammar school was founded at Taunton, chiefly for the tenants on the Bishop of Winchester's local estates; and in 1523, Bishop Fox, who also founded Corpus Christi College, Oxford, refounded it as Bishop Fox's Grammar School in what are now the municipal buildings. After flourishing in the eighteenth century, it declined to 20 boys by 1850. It was taken over by a company in 1867, renamed Taunton Collegiate School and moved to the former Mountlands Race Course, a site of 15 acres on the lower slopes of the Black Down Hills, south of the town. The new buildings—tower, dormitories, assembly hall, dining hall and Headmaster's house—were erected in a Gothic style by 1869. It had, however, few pupils, and the governors quarrelled with the remarkable Headmaster, the Rev. W. Tuckwell (later called the 'Radical Parson'), who erected the first room in any school for the teaching of science. He resigned in 1879, and the school was soon empty and bankrupt.

Woodard bought it for £8,000 from the mortgagee. It was opened in October 1880 on the thousandth anniversary of the death of King Alfred (whose camp at Athelney was near to Taunton), and named after him, though it was known popularly as King's College; but agricultural depression affected its numbers, which were 40 in 1882 (including 22 day boys), rose to 59 by 1886, but fell to 44 in 1890. Woodard supervised it himself, but was too tired and busy elsewhere to do this effectively.

After his death, numbers fell further to 21 in 1896, when it was closed, but it was reopened the next year on the establishment of the Western Division (see p. 97) with a new Headmaster, five masters and 14 boys. Numbers rose to 42 within a few months and to 120 by 1902. Three of the four big dormitories were occupied in the summer of 1898 and the fourth the following term. This made further building possible. In 1899 a new wing (including the library) was added to the west cloister, and the chapel was begun, but lack of money prevented its completion. Sport was encouraged by the extension of the sports fields southwards (1906) and construction of a swimming bath (1911).

Numbers rose during the First World War, reaching 178

in 1919, but then the economic depression reduced them to 147 by 1927. The college faced closure in 1930 when the chaplain, the Rev. P. M. Taylor, became Headmaster at a drastically reduced salary, and by employing local clergy-men as part-time teachers, persuading friends to join the staff virtually without payment and raising £2,000 in 1933 'to ensure the school remaining open for another year', he overcame the crisis in three years.

Dr R. D. Reid (Headmaster 1934–7) far-sightedly sold some land for house-building to buy an extra 50 acres adjoining the sports fields and extended the chapel east-wards in 1936 to complete its length. His successor, R. C. Unmack (1937–65), began with 216 boys, and numbers also increased during the Second World War, being 290 in 1945. Government restrictions rather than finance checked new building. A partial solution was to buy (between 1944 and 1966) several substantial houses, which had been built along South Road at the same time as the college build-ings, and also Fullands House (1946) and Pyrland Hall (1952) for a junior school (see p. 102). By 1955 building was possible and began as numbers rose from 320 in 1969 to 512 in 1979. Among the facilities added was better pro-vision for science and music. The college now has two theatres and an excellent art and design theatre, as well as a sophisticated video reproduction unit. The purchase of St Joseph's Convent on the opposite side of South Road (which closed in 1978) gained valuable new buildings, and

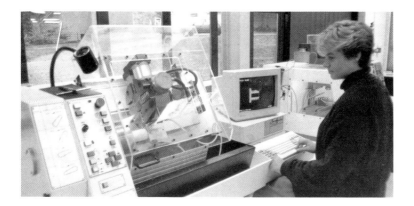

an artificial grass hockey pitch was made in its grounds.

In 1969 J. M. Batten (Headmaster 1968–88) said that his aim was 'to allow each individual boy as much freedom of choice as we can possibly manage, but at the same time to maintain a high standard of behaviour all round'; and he effected many changes. Tweed jackets replaced blue blazers, and informal leisure wear was allowed at weekends. Social rooms were introduced, and a beer bar provided for seniors; in 1971 the marshalled procession from house assembly points for meals ended when a cafeteria system replaced fixed seating in the dining hall. Two girls were admitted, as forerunners, to the VI Form in 1968; and a house was opened for day boys in 1982.

The college now has over 400 boarders and a day boy house of 60, including a VI Form of 200 of whom 50 are girl boarders. It has a house on Exmoor for weekend walking and relaxation; and it organizes exchange parties with the Institution Frémont at Lisieux. Among recent activities are Community Service, including caring for the gardens of the elderly, and a Conservation Group, which manages Thurlbear Wood, a local nature reserve.

Another stage in the school's progress came in 1928 when it was taken over by the Woodard Corporation from the High School Company and given its present name. St Clare was the thirteenth-century foundress of the Poor Clare nuns, and there was a medieval chapel dedicated to her near Polwithen. The school chapel (built in 1918) was now enlarged, largely through the efforts of the pupils, whose further help was urgently needed when the school suffered a serious gas explosion in 1930; they succeeded through fairs and plays in raising enough money for the installation of electric lighting by 1935.

The Second World War affected the school seriously. Though at first the area was thought to be safe, it prepared for the worst, asking all parents to contribute a guinea towards the cost of building an air-raid shelter, either by a lump sum or by instalments. Between 1940 and 1942 it shared its sports fields and laboratories with St Michael's School, which was evacuated from Sussex (see p. 53); but bombing spread to the West Country, and numbers declined, until by 1942 there were only 22 day girls and 48 boarders. In 1943 Miss M. Hudson became Headmistress. When Headmistress of St Elphin's School, Darley Dale, she had brought it through severe difficulties (see p. 94). During her three years at St Clare's, she raised the numbers to 183 and restored its financial stability.

Despite post-war problems, the school has made further progress. New buildings include three classrooms and an art room (1956), new laboratories (1963), a gymnasium and hall (1974) and music, needlework, and pottery rooms (1980). The chapel (further enlarged in 1956) is used for daily worship, and the boarders go to the parish church on Sundays. The VI Form has its own boarding wing with study bedrooms and a common room. There are about 80 boarders, 125 day girls (60 in the junior school) and 40 junior day boys.

The VI Form takes an 'Understanding Industry' course. There is provision for pupils who are dyslexic and for Eng-

lish as a foreign language. Under the present Headmaster, Ian Halford, there has been a growth in extra-curricular activities, including sailing, riding, archery and dancing, and with an emphasis on outdoor pursuits, the school has done well in the Duke of Edinburgh's Award Scheme and takes part in expeditions on Dartmoor. In 1990 it obtained a grant of £40,000 from the Wolfson Foundation for the development of arts and craft facilities. It is a small, happy school in surroundings of unique beauty.

# The Cathedral School

## LLANDAFF

The only Welsh choir school, it is situated near the Cathedral in the city of Llandaff, about two miles north-west of Cardiff. Like most such schools, it is of ancient origin. The Cathedral had a 'scholasticus' in the ninth century; in Mary's reign there were singing men and six 'queresters;' and in Elizabeth I's the Chapter paid £12 to a schoolmaster. Seventeenth-century Chapter records mention small payments to boys before and after the Commonwealth, but by 1691, when the Chapter was impoverished and the Cathedral ruinous, the singers were abolished, though the Chapter still had a small free day school in a room over the Chapter House, whose boys sang in the Cathedral.

It was refounded in 1880 in the old Deanery on the Cathedral Green by Charles John Vaughan, Dean of Llandaff and formerly the Headmaster of Harrow School, who had raised its numbers from 80 to 470, as a preparatory school for the 20 choristers and other boys. Under the continued direction of the Dean and Chapter, it grew in size, became a Woodard school in 1957 and the next year moved to the old Bishop's Palace, a large Georgian house

106

nearby with a small, pleasant chapel, standing in spacious wooded grounds and next to its sports fields of 11 acres. It now has a junior and pre-preparatory school, and its buildings include a gymnasium, swimming pool and science room. The Gloucester building housing 6 classrooms was opened by the Duke of Gloucester in 1987. In August 1990 fire destroyed the Pre-Prep department, subsequently rebuilt.

Its boarders still include the 20 Cathedral choristers, but its numbers have continued to grow, and girls were admitted in 1978. It is now the largest choir school in Britain. Its pupils between the ages of 4½ and 13½ consist of some 45 boarders, 220 senior and 100 junior day pupils and 120 pre-preparatory pupils. Dean Vaughan called it 'the darling of his heart', and it fulfils the religious and educational ideals he set before it, now strengthened by its membership of the Corporation.

# *Grenville College*

## BIDEFORD

In 1954 Walter F. Scott founded a boys' boarding school in buildings (vacated by West Bank School for Girls, which moved to Sidmouth) on high ground overlooking the historic port of Bideford on the river Torridge. He named it after the Elizabethan sailor, Sir Richard Grenville, a native of the town. As its first Headmaster, he sought to offer pupils opportunities, which he had not derived from his own conventional public school education.

In 1957, when it had 150 boys, he bought Moreton House with 40 acres of land about half-a-mile from the main premises. This mansion belonged to the Stucley family, who pioneered trade with America in the seventeenth century, and was rebuilt in 1824. The stables (the clock of which used to summon the family to morning prayers at 8.45 and to dress for dinner at 7.30) have been adapted for metalwork, art, pottery and woodwork. Among additions to the original buildings are a library, science and language laboratories and a multi-purpose chapel.

This acquisition enabled Scott to accept 70 new boys. He retired in 1964, and the next year the Woodard Corporation took over the college, which then had 255 boarders and seven day boys. His successor, John Crabbe, inaugurated in 1969 a dyslexic unit to meet the need professionally of the many boys with reading difficulties that it already had. Now it has six full-time teachers and about half the boys are entered as dyslexic. They are taught in small groups, but also attend classes and take part in sports with other boys. Boys taking this course have gone on to the universities. A recent research project undertaken in the Unit has resulted in the publication of several academic papers. Two new boarding houses, called Scott and Crabbe, were built in his time.

There are now 290 boarders and 75 day boys. It has been called 'an unusual, but not a special school'. It educates boys with and without difficulties, and it teaches English as a foreign language. It offers 24 GCSE and 18 A Level courses. Its position affords access to country, sea and town, which enables it to offer 15 sports ranging from

rugby and hockey to swimming and sailing. Skiing trips are organized and expeditions as far as Iceland. An unusual feature are the 29 clubs, run by the staff, which meet twice a week, and boys choose such activities as drama, electronics, ceramics or shooting.

There is a resident chaplain and a Sung Eucharist in the chapel on Sundays, while the parish church seats 800 for the annual carol service and confirmation service. There are strong links between the school and the town. The boys undertake voluntary social service work, and the Bideford Youth Orchestra and local clubs and societies use the school's facilities. Since 1978 St Andrew has been its patron saint, and coincidentally it now has an exchange scheme with St Andrew's School, Sewanee, Tennessee, an American Protestant Episcopal school.

# St Margaret's School

## EXETER

Miss Bessie Jago founded a school in Southernay West, Exeter, in about 1904 for 'the daughters of gentlemen'. She and her pupils dressed alike in Edwardian-style dark ankle-length skirts, white blouses and coloured ties. There were about 50 day girls and 12 boarders, who attended classes from nine to five o'clock each weekday. The main subjects were English and French literature, music and sketching and later science for the elder girls. Teaching methods included shutting a girl in a cupboard, who had to ask in French to be released. Tennis and cricket were played, but hockey was excluded as 'unladylike'.

In 1917 the school moved to its present site on the crest of a hill a mile from the centre of the city, where it now has seven large Georgian-style houses; and in 1920 Miss Jago sold it to Miss Winifred Edmonds. As Headmistress she successfully widened its scope and activities. Numbers increased to about 300, including about 30 boarders, and its buildings were extended. It survived the air-raid on Exeter in 1942 when staff-firewatchers extinguished incendiary bombs as they fell, but it lacked water, gas or

111

electricity for several days, and the boarders had temporarily to go elsewhere.

On her retirement in 1952 Miss Edmonds sold the school to a limited company under the Dean of Exeter. In 1968 it became an associated Woodard school and was taken over by the Corporation in 1975. Miss Frances Morford (Headmistress 1960–84) said, 'The educational standards demanded by the Corporation and the strength which results when schools of like interest are able to plan and work together offer an exciting promise for the future'.

This has proved so in many ways. Further new buildings include a science block (1964) and an assembly/dining hall (1972). Weekly boarding was introduced in 1961 and replaced full boarding in 1970. There are now about 450 girls including 65 weekly boarders. Sixth Form numbers have increased from three in 1960 to about 70, who have a separate common room and cooking facilities.

Higher academic standards have been accompanied by widening extra-curricular activities, which include expeditions on Dartmoor and to Iceland and the Young Enterprise Scheme, in which girls produce and market commercial products. The school has built up an outstanding musical tradition with choirs, orchestras and instruction in every musical instrument, enabling pupils to continue their studies in music colleges and universities. It also has an exchange scheme with St Andrew's School, Tennessee (see p. 151).

In its early days the proximity of Exeter School caused it difficulties. Girls were forbidden to speak even to their brothers when passing the games field, and wallpaper on the bottom half of its windows protected them from gazing boys, but both sides managed to communicate by hiding notes behind a loose brick in a wall. Miss Jago

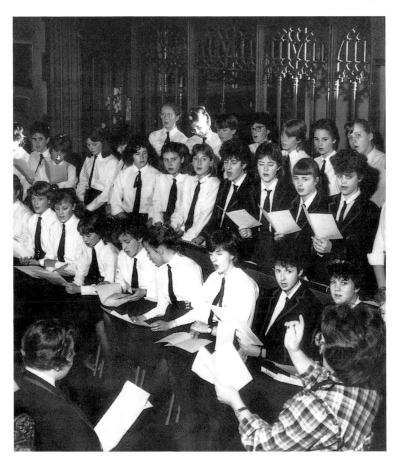

expelled a girl for buying sweets at Exceter School's tuckshop. Since 1975, however, the two schools have increasingly co-operated. They have the same full-time chaplain and a combined Christian Union; their VI Forms have been integrated for many subjects; they share the Music Centre; and some 40 girls have joined with the boys in the Combined Cadet Force. Changing times have turned a problem into a development, which has brought unique advantages to the pupils.

# The Northern Division

Late in the nineteenth century, the Midland Division decided to extend its activities to the east coast, and in 1901 Henry Edmund, 14th Viscount Mountgarret, secured a site and buildings for a girls' school just below Oliver's Mount on a hill above Scarborough. A local committee was formed, which in 1903 became the Northern Division as the Society of SS Mary and Aidan of York and took it over as Queen Margaret's School.

The first Provost of the Division was William Foxley Norris, later Dean of York and of Westminster successively, and he held the office until his death in 1937. He was succeeded by Eric Milner-White, Dean of York, who died in 1962. During that time the Division opened two more girls' schools—Queen Ethelburga's (1912) and Queen Mary's (1925)—both in Yorkshire, and in 1959 acquired the King's School, Tynemouth, the first Woodard day school and now the Corporation's largest school. In 1987 Elmslie Girls School, Blackpool, which is the only independent school in the country owned by a diocese, became associated with the Division. The Division now has a fulltime Secretary and Registra.

# Queen Margaret's School

## ESCRICK PARK, YORK

Miss Agnes Body (Headmistress 1901–13) was persuaded to take charge of the school by her friend, the Lady Warden of St Anne's School, Abbots Bromley. The daughter of George Body, canon of Durham and a noted missioner, she was then Headmistress of Lincoln High School. By her wish it was named after Margaret, sister of Edward Aetheling, wife of Malcolm Canmore and mother of three successive Scottish kings.

It began with seven girls, who slept in a room divided by sheets for cubicle curtains and had meals at one end of the dining-room and lessons at the other. Numbers grew steadily, and when the Old Margaretian Association was formed, the school welcomed it with equal concern for propriety and comfort: 'Low evening dresses are not worn, and please remember that the O.M. gatherings *always* bring a sea-fret and be prepared with warm clothing accordingly.'

Winifred Holtby, the novelist, who was a pupil at the

school from 1909 to 1916, described how German warships shelled Scarborough at breakfast time on 16 December 1914. The principal boarding house and St Martin's Church, used for school services, were hit, but the girls escaped unharmed along a route prepared for such an emergency and were sent home by train. The school reassembled at the Atholl Palace Hotel at Pitlochry in Scotland, until returning to Scarborough at Easter 1919.

During the following years many additions were made to its buildings, the most important being an educational block comprising classrooms, assembly hall, laboratories, art rooms and a domestic science wing, which was opened in 1932. The school also sought to help others less fortunate than itself. In 1919 it adopted the Shadwell Infant Welfare Centre in the London Docks, maintaining a trained nurse there and knitting childrens' garments during Lent. The Borough of Stepney took over the Centre in 1970.

In 1940 the school was evacuated to Castle Howard, the Palladian mansion built for Charles Howard, 3rd Earl of Carlisle by Vanburgh. The girls slept on iron bedsteads with their cloaks beside them in readiness for air-raids. In 1940 a fire gutted one wing of the great mansion. Staff and girls escaped, hurriedly dressed in odd collections of garments and carrying such possessions as they had rescued in their hands because most of their suitcases had been burnt. The insurance company, however, enabled growing girls to get better-fitting clothes than the war had hitherto allowed.

On 18 March 1941 the school buildings at Scarborough were wrecked by a land-mine; and after the War, the Chapter removed the school to Escrick Park, six miles from York, an Elizabethan country house (originally owned by Sir Thomas Knyvet, who discovered the Gunpowder Plot, arrested Guy Fawkes and secured his confession of guilt), which was extensively remodelled in 1758 by the well-known York architect, John Carr, and has 50

acres of parkland. In 1986, after the formation of a new company, it became an Associated school of the Woodard Corporation.

New extensions have been made, including the art and design centre (in the restored mill-house), home economics department, music department and a riding school. There is also an indoor swimming pool and a nine-hole golf course. The whole school worships in a new multi-purpose hall and chapel, and there is a Lady Chapel for quiet prayer. There is notable parental involvement in organization, work experience and other areas of school life. There are presently 261 boarders and 46 day girls. The VI Form of 18 have study-bedrooms in a group of converted cottages.

# Queen Ethelburga's School

## HARROGATE

When the Division wished to found another girls' school, Viscount Mountgarret offered it a site of 20 acres on condition that it was not 'just this site or that', but rather 'the best site that could be found in Yorkshire, if it were in the market'. It chose land on the moorland slopes above Harrogate, and he paid for the first stage of the building and gave the chapel. The school, named after the Queen who brought Christianity to the north in the seventh century, opened in 1912 with the advantage of new, purpose-built premises.

It started with 12 girls under Miss E. L. Young (Headmistress 1911–50), who chose its motto *Luce Magistra* and the Flying Eagle emblem. There were 50 girls (able to fill the north aisle of the chapel) when, on the first Speech Day on 21 October 1913, the ceremony of 'The Twelve' was begun by the first 12 pupils, who each wore a letter of the school motto; and now the 12 senior girls do this, the wearer of 'L' proposing the toast of Queen Ethelburga at the dinner.

During the First World War, each form adopted a prisoner of war, sending him a fortnightly food parcel. In the 1920s a connection was established with the diocese of Melanesia, and part of the annual charity bazaar's proceeds are still sent there. The school's twenty-first birthday in 1932 was marked by the opening of additional buildings, and by 1938 its numbers were 138.

In 1939 its buildings were requisitioned by the army. It moved in 52 furniture vans to the Queen Anne mansion of Studley Royal, some two miles from Ripon, and used Fountains Hall, near the Abbey, as a sanatorium. On 12 April 1946, when the school had packed everything to return to Harrogate, fire gutted Studley Royal. It lost possessions of all kinds, including 18 pianos, which were particularly difficult to replace.

The substantial buildings, left by the army after the War, were put to educational use, and new buildings have been added, including an art and design centre and a VI Form centre. Its junior department for girls between seven and eleven years (which was transferred to Queen Mary's

School in 1925) was re-established in 1982, and day girls are now admitted. There are now 150 boarders (each with her own bedroom) and 65 day girls, including 40 VI Formers. Music, art and drama are very active, and the school has an outstanding record in the Duke of Edinburgh's Award Scheme.

1991 marks the date of the transfer of the school, re-named Queen Ethelburga's College, to new ownership and to a new site, Thorpe Underwood Hall, situated midway between York and Harrogate.

123

# Queen Mary's School

## BALDERSBY PARK

In 1925 the Division established a girls' preparatory boarding school in the early eighteenth-century mansion of Duncombe Park, near Helmsley. A member of the staff of Queen Margaret's School, Miss Winifred Wright, was Headmistress from 1925 to 1933 and adopted the 'Four Cornerstones of the School: Trustworthiness, Hard Work, Public Spirit, Good Manners'. It began with 11 girls and 12 young girls from Queen Ethelburga's School (the 'Flying Eagles'), who came for a term 'to establish the Queen Ethelburga standard'. By 1926 its numbers had increased to 59. In 1931 it was announced, 'The King has been pleased to command that the School of Duncombe Park shall in future be known as Queen Mary's School.'

During the winter of 1939–40 the water and gas pipes froze in a foot of snow, and the school 'experienced all the items of the Benedicite'. When an army camp was established in the grounds, censorship prevented the publication of the school magazine from 1942 to the opening of the Second Front in 1944. The school adopted a Commonwealth prisoner of war and sent five guineas to supply him with cigarettes, books and games. At the end of the

war it had 72 boarders and three day girls. In 1979, while remaining a preparatory school, it established also a senior school for girls between 13 and 16, who are prepared for VI Forms and other educational courses.

When the lease of Duncombe Park expired in 1985, the school moved (in two containers a day for three weeks) to the fine Palladian mansion of Baldersby Park, near Thirsk, in 40 acres of grounds. The joint principals, Mr and Mrs Belward, had a colossal task to transform the house from its use as a country club divided into 35 holiday apartments; but now, to quote a magazine article, 'dignified main rooms lead on to modern classrooms'. The garages have become light, airy classrooms and the stables 17 music studios. Among new buildings are three laboratories, a gymnasium, swimming pool and an imaginative chapel. The choir sings in joint productions with Ampleforth College. There are some 220 pupils including 15 day girls.

# The King's School

## TYNEMOUTH

During the later part of the eighteenth century, stage coaches and turnpike roads brought growing numbers of visitors to Tynemouth, where in 1760 John Baker, Mayor of Newcastle upon Tyne, erected Tynemouth House as an occasional seaside residence. Its architect was James Paine, who also designed the Mansion House at Doncaster.

In 1867 the Rev. Thomas White moved his school, which he had founded in 1860 at Jarrow, originally for the sons of the Manager of Palmer's Shipyard, to Tynemouth House. It then had 12 boys, which rose to about 110 by 1890. The school was confined to Tynemouth House (now the Headmaster's residence), in which there were three classrooms furnished with desks each seating four or six boys, until 1922 when L. G. W. Wilkinson (Headmaster 1919–34) added a new wing and increased its numbers to about 200, founding a preparatory school in 1928 and a kindergarten in 1934.

When E. G. Ellison (Headmaster 1934–59) wished to sell the school, Kenneth Boddy, vicar of Holy Saviour's Church, Tynemouth, asked Malcolm Nicholson, archdeacon of Doncaster and a former vicar of St George's, Cullercoats, whether the Woodard Corporation would buy it. Dean Eric Milner-White wanted the Division to have a boys' day school, and when he heard of this, he persuaded the Corporation to take it over. Then aged 74, he gave much of the last four years of his life to the school, and his benefaction included the magnificent Provost's Gate, the main entrance to the school. He was supported by Noel Hudson, the Bishop of Newcastle, who said that such a school was 'the only possible way of catering for many of the people that the Founder had in mind.'

When the Corporation acquired the school in April 1959, Nicholson was appointed Headmaster, and it was named the King's School after the seventh-century King Oswin, who is said to be buried in Tynemouth, where there was a shrine to him. Of its 341 boys aged from five to eighteen, 262 were under 12 and only 79 in the top age

group including 11 in the VI Form. It had an overdraft of £35,000 and no endowment. In 10 years the top group grew to 310 and the VI Form to 64. Some £100,000 had been spent on buildings, which included a chapel and new science laboratories.

Girls were admitted in 1968 to the VI Form, which numbered 150 by 1980. The junior department has now 180 pupils aged four to eleven years, including girls from four to six years, and the senior school has 680 pupils. The construction of the Metro railway has enabled it to draw pupils from a much wider area than before. It has acquired old schools at Howick (on the coast) and Alnham (in the Cheviots) as centres for fieldwork in biology and geography in term-time and for expeditions during the holidays. Increasingly important are its links with local industrial firms, which have been able to influence closely classroom and laboratory teaching and strengthen its relations with the business and commercial world.

# *Elmslie Girls' School*

## BLACKPOOL

'We began in 1918 with eleven girls, three teachers, but no shortage of ideas or ideals,' so wrote the daughter of the Borough Surveyor, Miss Elizabeth Brodie, of the school she founded in a church hall in Blackpool. She was Headmistress until 1952 and was for many years assisted by her sisters, Miss Peggie and Miss Polly, who were respectively cook-housekeeper and matron-gardener. Four years later it moved to the Elms, a house built in 1896 and changed its name from Ellerslie School to Elmslie Girls' School. The grounds were full of purple and gold crocuses, which were adopted as the school colours. It then had 152 pupils, including about 20 boarders, who slept in a room on the first floor on the right of the staircase, which was separated by a dressing-room from Miss Brodie's bedroom, an area now occupied by the library. There were both girls and boys in the preparatory department.

Miss Brodie at first taught scripture, Latin, history and English and was remembered for her frequent injunction, 'Never end a sentence with a preposition,' as well as for her love of fresh air, which resulted in shivering classes being taught by her out on the lawn. Miss Peggie taught

cookery, and Miss Polly took classes to the municipal swimming bath and gymnasium. Miss Brodie soon initiated the 'Thursday Evenings', when she and the staff invited girls in turn to a social entertainment. The school became a centre for the Cambridge Local Examinations in 1924; the first Higher School Certificate pass was gained in 1928 and the first open university scholarship in 1932.

During the Second World War, the girls spent their spare time knitting socks and weaving camouflage material. It became entirely a day school in 1941 and ended the war with 353 pupils. In 1946 it entered upon what Miss Brodie called 'the second volume of its history', when it was taken over by the Blackburn Diocesan Board of Finance as a grammar and junior school; and it became an associated Woodard school in 1987. This unique combination has given the church in the Fylde area a school valued for both its religious influence and its academic standards.

It now has just over 400 pupils and includes a nursery and infant department. New buildings added to the original house include a gymnasium and assembly hall (1938), more classrooms in the Fisher block (1952), a chapel (1959) and VI Form Centre and music rooms (1988). Technology has been given an increasing part in the curriculum, and home economics and fashion and textiles are particularly strong areas. A recent annual event in the spring is the 'Elmslie Fashion Spectacular', a combined display of music, drama and fashion presented and modelled by the pupils. To the hockey and netball played in the winter and rounders and tennis in the

summer have been added badminton (1931), squash (1974), cricket (1980) and cross-country running (1980).

The importance of the chapel in school life is shown by the appointment of a Head Girl (Administration) and a Head Girl (Chapel). There are prayers every morning and special services each term. The pupils have always contributed generously towards charities, particularly the Church of England Children's Society, so putting into practice Miss Brodie's belief that 'no school can be alive which does not think of and work for others'.

# The Eastern Division

In 1895 Lowe, then Provost of Lancing, when asked about founding an Eastern Division replied, 'The present would not be a favourable moment to undertake work in a new division in East Anglia'; and in 1917 the Provost of the Midland Division declined an invitation from the eastern counties to open a girls' school there. Thirty years later, however, a special Corporate Chapter of the Woodard Corporation agreed on 29 May 1947 to set up a Council to take steps to form a new Divisional Society to be the Eastern Division of the Corporation, comprising the dioceses of St Albans, Peterborough, Ely, Norwich, Lincoln, St Edmundsbury and Ipswich, and Chelmsford. The Corporate Registrar wrote to 11 men (mostly clergymen) inviting them to join a Council of East Anglia for this purpose.

This Council first met on 7 November 1947 and three years later proposed the Society of SS Mary and Edmund of Bury St Edmunds 'to consist of men and women in sympathy with the purposes of the Founder'. But a Divisional Society could not exist without a school. At last Canon Alfred Woodard bought Cawston Manor for a school. Cawston College was opened as an associated school in 1964. Westwood House, Peterborough (now Peterborough High School), became another associated school in 1966, and so did St James' School, Grimsby, in 1968.

When Westwood House was incorporated in 1968, the Eastern Division could be constituted at Peterborough on 19 February 1968, with Aubrey Aitkin, archdeacon of Norwich, as the first Provost of Bury St Edmunds, and West-

wood House School was taken over. While St James'
School was incorporated in 1985, Cawston College
remains an associated school; the Divisional Chapter
meets at each in turn, giving all three equal attention.
Although the Division is the newest and smallest, it dis-
plays a fenlike determination to ensure its continuance
which may explain why it secured its original formation.

# Peterborough High School

PETERBOROUGH

In 1895, Peterborough High School, a girls' day school, was founded by a Miss Hill. At its annual Spring Festival on 22 March 1935, the Headmistress, Miss Mansfield, announced its immediate closure because of an unexplained 'delay of two years in expected help'. This was a great loss to the city, as its only other girls' secondary school, the County School, had only 60 places a year.

Surprisingly, the school premises were bought for an Educational Property Trust by the Misses Evelegh and Willcocks, who announced that it would reopen in September 1936. The new Headmistress, Miss Somerville, began the term with six girls, an assistant mistress and a daily maidservant. In January it was moved to 'spacious new premises with ample grounds at Westwood House, Thorpe Road'. By July Miss Somerville had engaged a science mistress and had 24 pupils, all day girls aged seven to fourteen in three classes, but at the end of the summer term she and all her staff were dismissed.

After an advertisement in the national press Miss Helen Mattock (later Mrs Belgion) became Headmistress in August. The school suffered through the treatment of her predecessor, and she started with only seven pupils, an assistant mistress and a resident housekeeper, but by the end of 1937 there were 33 pupils and two assistant mistresses. Its two proprietors, who weekly received the school's garden and greenhouse produce, gave it financial support to supplement the pupils' fees, but in November 1937 they were charged at the Old Bailey with fraudulently converting money subscribed to the City of London Building Society, of which the Educational Property Trust was a subsidiary. Miss Willcocks alone was found guilty.

The school had 64 pupils in September 1938. Mrs Belgion resolved to save it. With the help of Colonel A. H. Mellows, a company was set up which paid £3,000 for the buildings and fittings of the school with eight acres of land. It had 72 pupils in September 1939 and 200 by 1949, mostly day girls with some weekly and termly boarders.

A post-war event was the establishment of the Westwood House Mountaineering Club (claimed to be the first in a girls' school), which made such ascents as Snowdon and Kinder Scout.

After Mrs Belgion retired in 1961, the school was first associated in 1966 and then incorporated in 1968 with the Woodard Corporation. A new boarding house and a science and art block were built, and the old gymnasium in the stables (now the music block) was made in 1971 into the chapel of St Hugh of Lincoln, where all senior pupils attend a Holy Communion service. There has been a full-time chaplain since 1979, and an annual school confirmation is held in the Cathedral.

From the 1970s the rapid expansion of the city as a New Town brought the school rising numbers and further buildings, including home economics, chemistry, physics and art blocks and the extension and division of the boarding house into a junior and senior house. It has now some

380 pupils between the ages of 4½ and 18, including about 130 in the junior school. There are about 100 boarders in the senior school and 20 in the junior school.

Although there is a bias towards the arts, all girls do computer studies from the age of 11, and there is a varied curriculum. It is rare for any two VI Formers to be doing the same subjects, and four Science 'A Levels' may be studied. For a school established barely 50 years ago in unusually difficult circumstances, it has made remarkable progress.

For a number of years the school was known as West-wood House School, but in 1990 the Council of Governors, with the approval of the Woodard Corporation, restored the original name, Peterborough High School, thus acknowledging its links with the girls' private school founded in 1895 and identifying it more closely with the city of Peterborough.

# St James' School

## GRIMSBY

Grimsby, one of the oldest English boroughs, received its charter in 1202, when it was a prosperous port and built its large early thirteenth-century parish church of St James; but in the next century it rapidly decayed as its harbour silted up. A small stream at last was diverted in 1800 to form a new harbour, and it became an important fishing-port, when the railway came to the town in 1848 and constructed the Royal Dock. Its population spectacularly rose from 3,700 in 1841 to 63,000 in 1901. Now with nearly 100,000 it is by far the largest town in Lincolnshire.

As houses appeared on drained marshland, schools were needed too. The situation was one such as Woodard knew in Bethnal Green and Old Shoreham. National and other schools taught poor children, but private 'proprietory academies' provided for the middle-classes. Such was a boys' boarding-school established in Deansgate by Walter Lord Browne, formerly a master at Cranbrook School in Kent. Moved to Bargate in the early 1850s, it became important in the town, its pupils wearing mortarboards and Eton suits in church on Sundays.

This was also the time of religious revival in England.

The parish church was restored, a new organ was built, and choral services were started. From 1867 to 1879 an Oxford graduate, James Peter Young, was a curate there and then vicar until 1898. He shared Woodard's belief in education and music in worship. When he became vicar he wanted the parish church to have a choir school, like cathedrals, to give the choristers both musical training and a general education. In 1880 he established St James Choir School in the Aqua Rooms, an auctioneer's premises. When it succeeded, he wished to provide education also for the boys, when they outgrew the choir.

In 1882 Browne retired and sold his school to Young, who made it into St James' College, a day-school for the older boys. They had, advertisements stated, tuition in

book-keeping, art, football, daily drill, a hard playground and 'frequent opportunities for sea-bathing in season'. Later school rules stated, 'Catapults and articles of an inflammable nature must not be brought upon the premises'. As its patron, the Earl of Yarborough gave it a large number of books, which are still in the library.

The Aqua Rooms did not suit the Choir School, and Board Schools established under the Education Act of 1870 threatened both schools. In 1897, therefore, the Choir School moved to Bargate, and in 1904 more new buildings were provided there for the united school called St James' Choir School.

Since 1975 its name has been St James' School, but its link with the parish church remains. The choristers are educated there, receive a choral training and sing Evensong twice a week in the church as well as the services on Sundays and major festivals. The lay clerks and organist are connected with the school in various ways, and some ex-choristers sing in the choir as choral scholars.

The school has now purchased several more adjoining

large detached Victorian houses built in the prosperous part of the town during its rapid expansion, including Pelham House, so-called because it housed the Pelham School, a girls' school founded during the 1870s, which was closed in 1972. There is now a preparatory department founded in 1957 and a VI Form in 1959, so there are now pupils between four and eighteen years. Weekly boarders were taken in 1959 and termly boarders as well in 1964. Girls were admitted as day-pupils in 1973 and as boarders two years later. There are now about 170 day-pupils and 60 boarders in three Houses.

It became an associated Woodard school in 1968 and was incorporated in 1982, which involved the alteration of its constitution requiring its pupils to come from 'in and near Grimsby'. It lacks a chapel, but has a chaplain, and prayers are held on weekdays and Holy Communion during Lent, and pupils are prepared for confirmation. Every term begins and ends with a service in the parish church, which the boarders attend on Sundays. As a choir school and a Woodard school, it is faithful to the ideals of its original founders and of Nathaniel Woodard himself.

# Cawston College

## NORFOLK

Canon Alfred Woodard, the grandson of Nathaniel Woodard, wanted to establish a school to extend the work of the Corporation eastwards. After much searching, he and some friends bought at an auction in Norwich in October 1961 Cawston Manor, an Elizabethan-style country house, built by Sir Ernest George in 1896, with 125 acres of grounds, including woods, a lake and agricultural land, in countryside near the coast and the Broads. Here Cawston College was established as a boys' boarding-school and an associated Woodard school.

It opened in 1964 with John Asquith, who had taught at Bromsgrove School, as its first Headmaster. There were 43 boys, four assistant masters and a matron. The next year it had 90 boys, which had increased to 110 by 1968, but in 1971 there were only 45, and it seemed likely to close. It was largely saved by the Parents' Association, which still gives it valuable help. It now has 145 pupils, including 11 girls. It has recently become co-educational, and a girls' boarding house is being built.

Meanwhile, classrooms were built in 1966 and the library in 1969, to which were added an audio-visual room

143

in 1981, further classrooms in 1984 and a computer room in 1986. A riding-school building, given by a parent, was made into a gymnasium. There are two houses—younger pupils have dormitories and common rooms, the older ones bedsitters and studies.

A dyslexia unit was established in 1970, at which 70 pupils now receive help with reading, writing and spelling problems. English as a foreign language is also taught. Pupils follow a craft, design and technology course in their first three years and may continue it afterwards. It has a very rich ecological environment, which stimulates practical scientific work. Drama has been important from the beginning, and plays are performed with a local girls' school. Its grounds provide excellent opportunities for sport, and there is a Camping Club which has been to Snowdonia, Derbyshire, and Kenya. Pupils also participate in the Duke of Edinburgh's Award Scheme.

The former entrance porch of the Manor House has become a small chapel, seating about 20, where Holy Communion is celebrated. Morning and evening prayers are held in the new music room, and on Sundays, the pupils attend the parish church which is dedicated to St Agnes, now the school's patron saint.

The school shares much of the character of the first Woodard schools. It was established largely through the efforts of a member of the Founder's family as an act of faith, and it seeks to carry into the present time the original pioneering determination to provide a good boarding education with a religious purpose in a fine country house.

# The Corporation and the Schools today

Today there are 32 Woodard schools in a network spread through the country from Tynemouth to Penzance educating some 7,000 pupils. The Corporation forms the largest group of 'independent' Christian schools in Britain and possibly the world. It educates its pupils from nursery school to university level in a happy and disciplined environment, while stressing the importance of individuals and their need to develop their intellectual potential, self-discipline, compassion and tolerance; and it maintains, as many of their parents desire, the conviction of its founder that the tradition of Christian worship and common life is the basis of its purpose for them. They live in Christian communities, and many leave their school with a spiritual awareness which influences their lives. 'The fact that we centre on the Christian experience provides us with unity, purpose and rationale' (Grenville College).

Woodard himself believed that boarding schools best provided for the education of the whole child in body, mind and spirit, but today the Corporation's schools include day-schools and the others all take day pupils and in some cases, weekly boarders. The pattern of worship has changed, but the role of the chaplain in developing the religious life of the school is still vital. In every Woodard school there is a 'chapel', which remains the focus of the school. It may be like Lancing's awe-inspiring building

*Opposite: A Prestfelde pupil plans his day.*

147

or the Hereford Bluecoat School's imaginatively-designed dual-purpose classroom or Tudor Hall's intimate converted stable. Some schools have only weekday services; others find a conflict between 'leave weekends' and Sunday morning Eucharists. Such secular pressures, challenging a long-accepted practice of worship in the schools, originate in changing attitudes to boarding education. Pupils today come from a wider and more varied background than the middle classes whom Woodard envisaged. No longer are the schools' character and fees graded according to the social status of parents.

Some of the Woodard schools have participated in the assisted places scheme, which has enabled more parents to choose independent education for their children. A survey of boys' boarding schools in 1985 found that the parents of half of the pupils had not themselves been to such schools. Many parents now choose for their children boarding schools within easy reach of the family home. They expect that there will be during term-time some visiting days and leave weekends. If they live within 50 miles of the school, they can attend functions like confirmation and carol services, sports days and music concerts. They become more involved in the regular life of the school than past parents did. The growing demand for weekly-boarding and day-school places has coincided with problems of securing resident staff for boarding schools. Weekly boarding with four nights at school and three at home gives the pupils 'experience of valuable community living and yet maintains a secure family base' (St Margaret's School, Exeter).

Expectations of both parents and pupils for boarding education has brought financial problems for the Corporation. Its first boys' boarding schools had large dormitories, which have had to be adapted to provide the greater privacy and comfort expected today. Modern pupils desire individual study-bedrooms as work and social places.

The decline in demand for boarding education and rivalry from state VI Form colleges led from about 1980 to falling numbers in many boys' schools, which began to accept girls, at first as day pupils, but later as boarders as well. Most Woodard schools have taken girls at VI Form level only, but now a number are fully co-educational.

Parental pressure for examination successes, to lead to qualifications in the professions and industry, have brought many developments in the schools as the curriculum has changed. Woodard valued a classical education at a time when the public and grammar schools were beginning to teach science, astronomy, engineering and social science, and the Taunton Commission in 1868 held that 'the main study of the middle classes should be . . . some one or other of the physical sciences'. Lowe was ready at Hurstpierpoint to be more radical and experimental. He considered in 1857 submitting pupils to the newly-established Oxford Middle Class Examinations. Woodard forbade this, but finally adopted the idea of the inspection of all his schools by Oxford examiners. In the later part of the nineteenth century, many schools adopted a 'modern' side (emphasizing history, modern languages, mathematics and science) as well as a 'classical' side; and Henry Kemble Southwell, Provost of Lancing, encouraged the Woodard schools to follow their example (see p. 18). The introduction of the School and Higher Certificate examinations in 1917 standardized the secondary school curriculum and emphasized English subjects, foreign languages, science and mathematics, in which candidates had to satisfy the examiners.

Today the development of subjects like craft, design and technology has altered the teaching of home economics, domestic science, art and wood and metal work. Changes in the curriculum caused by the expansion of communications, the need for pupils to know about computers and the stress on languages to meet opportunities in Europe have required new arts centres, computer rooms and language laboratories. School sport reflects the stress on the individual and concern for physical fitness. Team sports like rugby and hockey are challenged by squash, fencing, golf and aerobics. Sports centres provide facilities for many sports and often have a dual role as a social centre for the school. Most schools have all-weather pitches to reduce interruptions to games.

Woodard schools have a long tradition of musical excellence, and new music centres and theatres have enhanced the opportunities to learn individual instruments, singing, dance and drama. Outside pressure for such new activities have brought fund-raising for new buildings to the forefront of school activities. Societies of past pupils have often taken an active interest in their school and generously raised money for it.

These societies also help schools in another vital way. As it is assumed that all pupils will have careers and seek a wider range of higher education, schools now provide advice and information about careers; and former pupils assist with lectures and contacts which make job sharing and work experience possible.

In the tradition of Nathaniel Woodard, schools have sought to meet the special needs of pupils. Among these are the dyslexic at Cawston College and Grenville College and physically-handicapped at the Hereford Bluecoat School. Schools have also responded to the changing curriculum and GCSE examination. They are now considering the influence on independent schools of the National Curriculum, with its assessment of pupils and detailed monitoring of performance, in state schools.

The Corporation itself has adapted to a changing world. To maintain the excellence of its schools, it is working towards better administrative, financial and human resource management at all levels by Corporate and Divisional chapters as well as schools, whose Heads are seen as managers as well as good teachers, and whose role in attracting pupils is increasingly important in the competitive world of independent schools. Its responsibility in determining overall policy has led the Corporate Chapter, aware of the rapid changes in education, to set up a working party under the direction of Sir Peter Laurence 'to review the present working of the Statutes of the Corporation in the light of the contemporary situation in Church and Society to ensure the better fulfilment of the Corporation's purpose'.

The Corporation continues its original purpose of promoting and extending education on Christian principles. It is now much more difficult than it was in the nineteenth century to raise money to found new schools, but over the years schools, sharing the Woodard ideal, have joined the Corporation as incorporated or associated schools. The Corporation's influence now extends more widely than originally intended and includes preparatory, choir and comprehensive schools. Overseas it has links with schools in Africa and the United States of America. A further extension of Woodard influence came in 1980 when Ian Beer, Headmaster of Lancing, was the first Woodard Chairman of the Headmasters' Conference.

Many Woodard schools have established close ties with their own local community. They provide employment and commercial opportunities for its people and may be able to offer the use of buildings such as sports centres and music and drama facilities. Some schools express their Christian commitment by providing choirs for local churches and helping the aged and handicapped.

The Woodard schools enjoy great freedom of management and initiative and are proud of their own characteristics and traditions. Sometimes this is expressed in the observance of old-established ceremonies, such as Jerusalem Heights, a tradition at the School of St Mary and St Anne, Abbots Bromley since its foundation, when the school, singing the long version of the hymn 'Jerusalem, my happy home', processes at the end of the summer term to the parish church for the Commemoration Service for girls who are leaving.

At the same time, the schools are part of a larger joint enterprise in which they support each other and together further the Woodard ideal. It is not easy for the Corporation to encourage a common corporate feeling among its scattered and diverse schools. It has tried to promote inter-school co-operation and encourage conferences for teachers and VI Formers in Woodard schools and sporting events, such as sports meetings and cricket festivals. There have been Woodard Newsletters and Woodard Lectures which have been subsequently printed, and schools have exchanged their magazines. The annual service in Lancing Chapel (see p. 18) is an occasion when the common foundation of the schools is demonstrated in an explicit way.

In 1982 all the schools joined in an impressive public demonstration of their corporate life at the week-end Woodard Festival in London, and some 2,000 people attended a concert in the Festival Hall and a service in Westminster Abbey. This made a great impression on those who took part in it—'Simply meeting people from other schools and seeing the banners gave a tremendous family feeling,' said one from St Margaret's School, Exeter. The words of another, from St Hilary's School, Alderley Edge, reflected the thoughts of many: 'It made me proud,' she said, 'to be a member of the Woodard Schools.'

# Index